Graham Crackers & Milk

To: Susan and Will,
I thank God for you
and for all you mean to all of us!
I pray my book will be
Food for *your* heart + soul.

Much love,
John Graham
and Pat, too
9. 7. 03

Graham Crackers & Milk

Food for the Heart & Soul

John K. Graham

DIMENSIONS
FOR LIVING
NASHVILLE

GRAHAM CRACKERS AND MILK
FOOD FOR THE HEART AND SOUL

This book is printed on elemental-chlorine-free paper.

Library of Congress Cataloging-in-Publication Data

Graham, John (John Kirkland)
  Graham crackers and milk : food for the heart and soul / John K. Graham.
    p. cm.
  IBSN 0-687-07472-X (pbk.: alk. paper)
  1. Christian life. I. Title.

BV4501.3.G734 2003
242—dc21

                                2003009291

All scripture quotations unless noted otherwise are taken from the New Revised Standard Version of the Bible, copyright 1989, by the Division of Christian Education of the National Council of the Churches of Christ in the United States of America. Used by permission. All rights reserved.

Scripture quotations marked (NIV) are taken from the HOLY BIBLE, NEW INTERNATIONAL VERSION®. NIV®. Copyright © 1973, 1978, 1984 by International Bible Society. Used by permission of Zondervan Publishing House. All rights reserved.

Scriptures marked (KJV) are from the King James or Authorized Version of the Bible.

Excerpt taken from FEARFULLY & WONDERFULLY MADE by PHILIP D. YANCEY and PAUL W. BRAND. Copyright © 1980 by Paul Brand and Philip Yancey. Used by permission of Zondervan.

03 04 05 06 07 08 09 10 11 12—10 9 8 7 6 5 4 3 2 1

Contents

Preface

Graham Crackers and Milk

❧❖❧

*W*hen I was a boy, every evening before going to bed my father would go into the kitchen for what he called a "midnight snack." It wasn't midnight—more like ten o'clock—but that was okay with me. My brothers may have snacked with us—I don't recall—but as for me, I treasured those few minutes at the end of each day as time for my father and me to be together.

My dad's midnight snack was a ritual. He would open either a can of Vienna sausages or a can of sardines. In those days the cans had a key attached that you could remove and use to unroll the lid. When I got older, Dad let me unroll the cans for him, cautioning me not to cut myself.

Along with the Vienna sausages and sardines, my dad ate soda crackers and drank a glass of buttermilk. I could not stand to smell the buttermilk, and I didn't think too highly of Vienna sausages because of the jelly in which they were packed. Nor did I care for sardines. They didn't taste anything like the catfish and perch we caught in our pond. They had a strange, wild flavor, I thought. My mother said I was a finicky eater, and she was right.

While Dad ate his snack, I had Graham crackers and a glass of milk. I thought it was neat that a cracker carried my family's last name. As for the milk, I drank only pasteurized milk that was refrigerator cold. We had several milk cows on our farm, but the moment I learned in school all the diseases you could get by drinking raw milk, I would have none of it. The very idea that my dad would allow our cow's milk to stand and clabber, and then drink it, was unthinkable to me. Fresh, cold milk from Jersey Gold Dairy was what I wanted. And Graham crackers.

The nightly ritual of eating with my father fed more than my body; it nourished my heart and my soul. It was the time I felt closest to my father. Often Dad would tell me what he had done that day and what he was going to do the next. I was the first in the family to learn these things, and I cherished them dearly.

Over time, Graham crackers and milk became a metaphor for me of relationship with God the Father. I envision the crackers as bite-sized bits of wisdom, and milk as richer nourishment from God's Word that can help us grow into the image of Christ. As the author of 1 Peter 2:2 says, "Like newborn babies, crave pure spiritual milk, so that by it you may grow up in your salvation, now that you have tasted that the Lord is good" (NIV).

Graham crackers and milk: food for the heart and soul. I believe this kind of nourishment comes best in the form of metaphors and stories. Jesus taught in parables and used metaphors in his teachings. Metaphors carry multiple layers of meaning. We can all identify with them—they touch our heart and soul with meaning deeper than can be fully expressed.

In 1990, after serving as a plastic surgeon for fifteen years, I left the practice of medicine, entered seminary, and eventually became a priest in the Episcopal Church. At my first church, St. Matthew's in Austin, Texas, I discovered that during my sermon preparation, when I meditated on Scripture, almost always stories would come to mind that gave the passage relevance for that setting. Usually, I would identify a metaphor, and as I looked at that metaphor, a prism of meaning would unfold.

To my pleasant surprise, people would always remember the metaphor that I had used. To this day, when I see people who have heard me preach or teach, they will say, "I will never forget the sermon about your mother's picture window"; or "I loved you telling us how you always wanted to be a good Samaritan; I always have too"; and "I will never forget the story you told about the time you were in the swimming pool and God said, 'I want you all the way in, not part-way in.'"

The power of the metaphor is that it can bypass our rational, logical, scientific mind and go straight to the unconscious realm of the heart and soul. I believe that's why metaphors speak to people of every faith and of every race, culture, and creed.

This is a book filled with metaphors: my mother's picture window, the pig I scrubbed to win a prize at the Louisiana State Fair, a storm, a fence, "in-between" time. I believe they communicate God's grace and can touch hearts. I pray that this book will touch your heart, as well.

In chapter 23, I mention that I had always wanted to be a good Samaritan and say that this has only happened in my life through the help of others. This is no less true in the writing of this book and for that reason, I must thank those who helped make it a reality. First, I must mention my wife, Pat, who gave advice and reflection on each chapter; my daughter, Cathey, who suggested my sermons would make a great book; and my agent and friend, Kathleen Niendorff. Without them, and others, this book never would have been published.

Chapter 1

My Mother's Picture Window

"As the Father has loved me, so I have loved you; abide in my love. If you keep my commandments, you will abide in my love, just as I have kept my Father's commandments and abide in his love. I have said these things to you so that my joy may be in you, and that your joy may be complete. This is my commandment, that you love one another as I have loved you. No one has greater love than this, to lay down one's life for one's friends. You are my friends if you do what I command you. I do not call you servants any longer, because the servant does not know what the master is doing; but I have called you friends, because I have made known to you everything that I have heard from my Father. You did not choose me but I chose you. And I appointed you to go and bear fruit, fruit that will last, so that the Father will give you whatever you ask him in my name. I am giving you these commands so that you may love one another." (John 15:9-17)

A window. That's all my mother wanted—a window. The window she wanted was a picture window for her living room. The request was not too great. My father was a building contractor in the 1950s and had crews of workers putting picture windows in all the houses he was building. People liked the idea, and his houses were selling well. Yes, a picture window was what people wanted. A picture window was what my mother wanted, too.

When I was in the second grade, my father and mother moved to the country a few miles outside of Shreveport. They bought land, dug a water well, and cut a long, winding road through trees and dense undergrowth to the highest point on this bit of hill-country land. I say "hill-country land," but this was Louisiana, not central Texas or Colorado. A small knoll or rise in the ground would be more descriptive—perhaps ten to fifteen feet higher than the rest of the land. On that tiny little hill my father built a small two-bedroom, one-bath house. It did not have a living room, only a glassed-in porch. Later they added two bedrooms and a bath, which allowed one of the former bedrooms to become a living room. The only problem was, it only had two small side windows.

My mother's joy was her flower garden. But from her living room she could not sit and view her beloved garden. A solid wall stood in the way. The answer was clear enough: A picture window was needed. Like the one my father advertised every day in the newspaper. That would do just fine.

Only, my father said no. He could not pull a work crew off the job to put a picture window in his own home. This was the first time my dad had made *real* money in years. Stop? *Now?* Pull men off the job, while houses were selling left and right? Never! It was unthinkable. Week after week my mother asked for the window, and week after week my father said no. One morning after an exchange of words, my mother pulled out a suitcase and began packing. "Leave if you want," my dad shouted. "No one is going to tell me what I have to do!"

Being a child ten years old, I was frightened. So I tried to talk my mom out of her demand for a window. She said, "If your dad loved me, he would do this. He only loves his work. All I want is a window so I can see my flowers."

Desperate now, I raced to my bedroom, got a piece of paper, and scribbled a drawing of the front of our house with a big picture window and my mother's flowers in the front yard. I hurried to catch my father as he was darting to his car. I said, "Dad, this is a picture of what Mom wants. You can do it for her. Can't you?" My dad never answered. He just stuffed the picture into his pocket and drove off in a cloud of dust. (It shouldn't surprise anyone to learn that as an adult, I had to learn not to be a "Mr. Fixit.")

I got on my school bus that morning not knowing if my mother would be there when I returned. But that afternoon, I arrived to find a great big gaping hole in the side of our house! Workmen were every-where, busy at work, and my dad was standing there directing the whole thing as if it had been his idea all along. My mother was water-ing her roses. She was radiant as I raced over and hugged her as tightly as I could.

I knew something had happened that day that was altogether amazing. My mother had risked everything in expressing her heart's desire for a window. A conflict had taken place, and miraculously it had been resolved. Love had won out. I marveled at the power of love to heal division, to make enemies become one.

The fifteenth chapter of John is the last of the long discourses in which Jesus makes a series of "I am" statements. Previously, Jesus had said, "I am the bread of life" (John 6:48), "I am the resurrection and the life" (11:25), and "I am the good shepherd" (10:11). Now, in this chapter, Jesus says, "I am the vine, you are the branches." He then says, "Those who abide in me and I in them bear much fruit" (15:5). The invitation is to come to Jesus himself. We are not invited to an ideology about Jesus, not a philosophy, not a creed, not a dogma. No, if I want to bear much fruit, I must abide in Jesus and in him alone.

The question is, How do I do that? How do I remain in Jesus? The answer is found in this passage. Jesus makes it clear that the issue is not how do we get God to love us. God *always* loves us, and God's love is unconditional, absolute, total, and complete. Jesus said, "As the Father has loved me, so have I loved you." So, the issue is not whether we can receive God's love; rather, the issue is how can we remain in Jesus and love others. To say it another way, God's love is unconditional, but our ability to remain steadfast and manifest Jesus' love to others is conditional. How can I do that? How can I show Jesus' love to others?

There are two things to consider. First, Jesus said, "If you keep my commandments, you will abide in my love" (John 15:10). Second, he said, "This is my commandment, that you love one another" (15:12).

As to the first condition, when Jesus said his audience was to keep his commandments, immediately his hearers in the early church would have been reminded of the Old Testament covenant between Yahweh—God—and his people. What is a covenant? A covenant is a legal contract that defines the conditions of the parties involved in relationship. It identifies the blessing one can expect by keeping covenant; it also defines the penalties for breaking it.

Love is like that. It is covenantal and relational. For me to abide in a covenantally loving relationship with you, there are conditions. I cannot ignore, use, abuse, manipulate, undermine, destroy, betray, deceive, exploit, or willfully harm you and think that I am abiding in love. God still loves me even while I do these things, but I am not abiding in the love of Jesus Christ when I lie to you, when I betray your trust, or when I gossip about you. In fact, I *break* my relational covenant with you when I do these things.

As for the second condition, Jesus said that if we are to abide in him, we must imitate him by loving "one another" (John 15:12). It is one thing to say we love people who live in a foreign land; in many ways, that's easy. It is an altogether different thing to love "one another"— those nearest you. That's where the rub begins. So, how do we do that? How do we love "one another"? Jesus said, "No one has greater love than this, to lay down one's life for one's friends" (John 15:13). That's how we imitate Christ—by putting ourselves aside long enough to hear what the other person is saying, long enough to recognize their need, long enough to hear their hurt and feel their pain. Then and only then can we begin to learn to love.

My father learned how to express his love for my mother that day. To do so, he had to lay himself aside, along with his desire to make more money, sell more houses. Only then could he begin to listen as my mother expressed her needs. Expressing our needs involves risk: My mother and father could have separated.

The risk was real enough. You see, my mother knew something I did not know until years later. She knew that my father had deserted his first wife and left her with six children, over very nearly the same type of altercation. "No one is going to tell me what I have to do!" he had said. And with that, he left his first wife. Indeed, my mother had risked it all.

Was she just trying to manipulate my father into getting what she wanted? I don't think so. I believe she was putting a condition before my dad. I believe she was saying, "If you want us to have a relationship, it must be built on love—a mutually beneficial one." For her never to have taken the risk may have meant never to have been loved.

Every person has legitimate needs. We all have the need for affirmation, for acceptance, for understanding, and for love; and for these needs to be met, we must express them. There is a risk that we will be rejected—as you already may know all too well; but there is also the opportunity that love will be returned.

After my mother got her picture window, I loved to sit in front of it and look out. Every winter I would watch the snowflakes fall. Every spring, if I looked to the left side, I could see a chinaberry tree covered with blossoms. Straight ahead were my mother's flowers, and to the right side I could see a huge climbing wisteria vine that completely covered a bent-over pine tree—one that seemed to bow down so we could easily reach the blossoms. For years, that vine was not even visible until my father had all the undergrowth hacked away. There it was as it had been all those many years—only hidden—a beautiful vine with its luscious purple flowers hanging so abundantly, so gracefully.

Many of us are like that. Year after year we sit in isolation, unable to have our heart's desire met—to be loved. Finally someone hears our cry for help and responds by opening a window into our life. Slowly the thicket surrounding us is hacked away. New treasures are found to the right and to the left, in every direction; blessings we never knew existed are found. Love is like that.

My father opened more than a window in a wall that day. He also opened the window of his heart—to my mother, and to God as well. You see, my dad's act of love affected every area of his personal and business life. As the years passed, he became a generous and loving human being. God also allowed him to become reconciled with the children he had once deserted.

For some people, this chapter may be far too personal—the telling of family secrets. If you are like that, it might help to know that contemporary theologian Frederick Buechner has said that we are never closer to God and to God's love than when we share our secrets. That being true, I will share one final thing about my dad. He lived two years longer than my mom, and every day he would say to me, "Son, losing your mother was like having half my heart ripped out." Quite a statement from a man who once had invited my mother to pack her bags.

I witnessed this amazing transformation take place in the life of my father. I know firsthand the miracles that love can do. Opening the windows of our heart to love others can bring about that kind of miracle in our lives too.

Chapter 2

The Full Sun

In the time of King Herod, after Jesus was born in Bethlehem of Judea, wise men from the East came to Jerusalem, asking, "Where is the child who has been born king of the Jews? For we observed his star at its rising, and have come to pay him homage. When King Herod heard this, he was frightened, and all Jerusalem with him; and calling together all the chief priests and scribes of the people, he inquired of them where the Messiah was to be born. They told him, "In Bethlehem of Judea; for so it has been written by the prophet: 'And you, Bethlehem, in the land of Judah, / are by no means least among the rulers of Judah; / for from you shall come a ruler / who is to shepherd my people Israel.'" Then Herod secretly called for the wise men and learned from them the exact time when the star had appeared. Then he sent them to Bethlehem, saying, "Go and search diligently for the child; and when you have found him, bring me word so that I may also go and pay him homage." When they had heard the king, they set out; and there, ahead of them, went the star that they had seen at its rising, until it stopped over the place where the child was. When they saw that the star had stopped, they were overwhelmed with joy. On entering the house, they saw the child with Mary his mother; and they knelt down and paid him homage. Then, opening their treasure chests, they offered him gifts of gold, frankincense, and myrrh. And having been warned in a dream not to return to Herod, they left for their own country by another road. (Matthew 2:1-12)

Before entering seminary to become a priest, one of my great joys was the lake house we owned in Shreveport, Louisiana. It was situated on Cross Lake, a beautiful lake just a fifteen-minute drive from my office. What I liked most was that every morning I could sit on my patio, wrapped in a warm blanket, a cup of hot coffee in my hand, and watch a glorious sunrise.

I found this to be a most exhilarating experience. In fact, I watched the sunrise enough times to discern four successive phases or stages that took place one after the other every single morning.

First, there was the stage of darkness, where the trees were just blackened silhouettes against a star-studded sky. Overhead, the giant pine trees were filled with cypress gnats. Cypress gnats look like giant mosquitoes, except they are friendlier. They don't sting you. The low-pitched hum of the millions of gnats captured the early morning hour. Stage one: the stage of darkness; the stage of gnats.

In the second stage, the darkened sky was replaced with a glorious display of pastel colors caused by the reflection of the sun's rays off the earth's atmosphere. Each morning was different. Sometimes the pink colors dominated; on other occasions, the orange or purple hues. For me, it was as if God painted the sky with a different palette every day. Often I would ask, "Lord, what colors are you going to use today?" And, along with the changes in the sky came a chorus of birds who replaced the gnats. Only a few at first, but soon every bird sang as loudly as its lungs would allow. Stage two: the stage of reflected light; the stage when birds begin to sing.

Stage three. In this stage, the sun's first rays appeared over the horizon and then danced their way across the water to greet me. And, with the sun, out came the animals. Soon, squirrels jumped from limb to limb, from tree to tree. A mother mink and her little ones would scamper at the water's edge. Dogs began to bark in the distance. Stage three: the stage of the sun; the stage when the animals came alive.

Finally, stage four. Just after the sun rose, I would hear off in the distance a high-pitched whine. Louder and louder it grew until suddenly, around a bend in the lake, a fisherman in a metal boat with a 120-horsepower outboard motor—turned up full throttle—would shatter the serenity of my morning. After the fisherman came the sound of chain saws, hammers, and trucks on a nearby road. Stage four. The stage of man, and I knew nothing would ever be the same.

I've taken all this time to tell you these details so that you will realize how much that early morning hour meant to me. And so you can also understand how much I wanted to share that experience with my family.

Each morning I would enter the house and try to entice at least one member of my family to join me in my five o'clock vigil. Always I received a resounding "No!" They thought it insane to get up that early in the morning just to see a sunrise.

Finally, one weekend my daughter Ginger invited a friend to stay with us. As soon as she arrived, I told her about the wonderful sunrise I had seen that morning. I also told her I couldn't get a single member of my family to join me, and to my complete shock, she said, "Dr. Graham, I'd love to see a sunrise. I've never seen one!"

The next morning Ginger's friend awoke at the crack of dawn to join me in viewing the glorious sunrise on Cross Lake. She loved it and a few days later mailed me a letter and a beautiful poem she had written to express what was for her an epiphany—a time in which she experienced God in the glory of God's creation—in the rising of the sun whose rays pierced the darkness of a cold night, bringing warmth and awakening her to a new day.

On another cold, dark night, wise men came to Bethlehem, where Christ's epiphany brought warmth to their hearts and awakened all humankind to a new day. The story is familiar, one that is full of mystery, to be sure, and yet full of power.

Scripture tells us that when the Christ Child was born in Bethlehem, the Magi saw a new star in the sky. They followed its light because they believed the appearance of a new star foretold the birth of a new king. First they visited another king—Herod the Great, King of Judah. But Herod's kingship was not by birthright. Although Herod was not a Jew, Rome had appointed him to rule. And Herod knew full well that he could be replaced at any moment. To maintain his power, Herod resorted to murder. The list of those who died is a long one: Herod's wife, his three sons, his mother-in-law, his brother-in-law, an uncle, and many others were killed so this man could remain in power.

Needless to say, Herod was troubled to learn of the coming of a newborn king, so he inquired where the child might be born. The scribes and chief priests quoted from the prophet Micah, who had prophesied that in Bethlehem one would be born who would shepherd the people of Israel. Bethlehem? Not to worry—just a tiny village. No one of importance had ever come from there. Still, better be safe.

So Herod asked the Magi to go and find the newborn king and then return to tell him, so that he might worship the child also. The Magi were guided by the star, and it led them to Bethlehem and a house where they found the child and his mother, Mary. The wise men

worshiped Jesus. And they presented him with gifts—gold, frankincense, and myrrh—just as foretold by the prophet Isaiah. Next, the
Magi were warned in a dream not to go back to Herod, so they returned
to their own country by another route. That is the story we have of the
wise men—the first Gentiles to whom Christ was revealed, the
Epiphany.

After my daughter's friend experienced the sunrise and wrote her
lovely poem, my family was shamed into joining me on the patio. First
came my younger son, ten-year-old Patrick, and a few weeks later my
wife, Pat, joined us for the morning ritual.

The three of us sat together on that chilly morning, wrapped in blan-
kets, Pat and I with mugs of piping-hot coffee in hand. As always I
loved to smell its wonderful aroma, taking sip after sip of a special
blend. In great detail I described for Pat each of my four stages in
observing the sunrise, as we began to experience them together in
order. The stage of darkness: cypress gnats and trees in blackened silhouettes. Then, the stage of birds, with the sky filled with glorious pink
hues, the sun reflected but not yet visible.

Then, it appeared—just a dot at first. A few moments later, there it
was, in all its glory—beaming brightly, rays dancing across the waters
to greet the three of us, to warm us. And oh, how blessed I was to share
this glorious moment with those I love! Precisely at that moment Pat
made her now-famous observation. She said, "Oh, isn't that nice. My
very first sunrise, and it's a full sun!"

"A full sun"? My son's head shot around to face mine and I turned
to face him. Neither of us could believe what we had just heard. "A full
sun"? What had she expected? A *half* sun? Perhaps a crescent-shaped
one?

I've thought a lot about my wife's observation, and I believe it is
spiritually significant, although that was doubtless not her sleepy
intent. The fact is, we Christians make a truly remarkable statement
when we say Jesus is "a full Son"—bright and shining for all who will
see, a full manifestation of God in all his glory.

Jesus is not like the moon; he is not a mere reflection of God's light.
In Christ we do not have just a quarter of God's glory, nor a half, nor
nine-tenths. No, in Jesus Christ, God was fully manifest, fully revealed.
The apostle Paul, in his letter to the Colossians, put it this way:
"[Christ] is the image of the invisible God. . . . For in him all the full-

ness of God was pleased to dwell, and through him God was pleased to reconcile to himself all things." (Colossians 1:15, 19-20).

The question is, do we know the Jesus who fully and perfectly reveals God in all God's glory? Or are we stuck in the stage of darkness, where we can hear only the drone of gnats overhead, see only a blackened silhouette? Or maybe we have seen Christ *reflected* in God's creation—bright and beautiful, but still only a reflection. Perhaps we see Jesus as a great teacher, but just one among many; not the real thing, not God.

But for many, Jesus Christ has risen, and they have seen God in all his glory. For these, just as I wanted to share the sunrise with my family, so they want to share with everyone the love of God as revealed in Jesus Christ.

Christians do not need to force people to accept Christ. We are comforted knowing the revealing of Christ is God's work, not ours. The Holy Spirit is constantly seeking to reveal Christ to all who will open their hearts to him. We can, however, reflect and tell what Christ has meant to us; every reflection of Christ is beautiful to behold.

My prayer is that Christ will be revealed to you. I pray that you may know Jesus as the one who reveals and manifests God to this world— God in fullness, with no shadow or turning. When that glad day happens—and it could happen this very day—when that happens for you, no one will have to explain it to you, because you will understand what Epiphany is all about.

And on that glad day, suddenly poetry and songs of praise will pour forth from our heart—just like they did for my daughter's friend. That's what happens when we—who once sat in darkness but now have come to God's marvelous light—like the chorus of birds, begin to sing in exultation, "Glory be to God on high, and Glory to his Son, Jesus Christ."

Chapter 3

Not Part-way, But *All* the Way In

I appeal to you therefore, brothers and sisters, by the mercies of God, to present your bodies as a living sacrifice, holy and acceptable to God, which is your spiritual worship. Do not be conformed to this world, but be transformed by the renewing of your minds, so that you may discern what is the will of God—what is good and acceptable and perfect. (Romans 12:1-2)

*O*wning a swimming pool means you must keep it clean—which isn't always easy, especially if your pool is covered by a huge, spreading oak tree as was the pool at our home in Shreveport. When the leaves began to fall from the oak tree, I spent many hours removing them. I soon learned that it was easier to dip the leaves off the top of the water than it was to let them settle to the bottom of the pool. So, I developed the habit of skimming leaves off the top of the pool three times a day. I would dip just before leaving for work and when I returned home. I often raced home at lunch too. If I was able to follow my three-times-a-day ritual, hardly a leaf made it to the bottom of the pool.

At the time, I was a physician and usually skimmed for leaves wearing the clothes I wore to work that day—suit, coat and tie. No problem, I thought. I could walk along the edge of the pool, skim off leaves, and never get wet. Except when accidents happened. On several occasions, I fell into the pool, would dash into the house wringing wet, and would put on a change of clothes before going to the office. It became a family joke—me falling into the pool, suit and all.

One day when I was home at noon, skimming the pool, I had laid down the skimmer and turned around to see it sliding into the pool. Immediately I tore off my coat and pushed the sleeves of my shirt up to the elbow. I thrust my hand into the water just as the pole slipped past my fingertips and floated to the bottom of the pool. I stood in disgust for a few minutes pondering my predicament. Finally, I determined, *If I'm going to clean the leaves off the pool, I need the skimmer.* So, looking around and seeing no one looking my way, I slipped off my shirt and pants and slid into the water in my underwear.

At first I tried to reach the pole by keeping my head above the water, so as not to mess up my hair. Realizing this was not possible, I thought, *If I am going to clean the leaves, I have to have the skimmer, and to get the skimmer, I am going to have to go all the way under.* Having decided that, I thrust my head under the water; and when my hand grasped the pole of the skimmer at the bottom of the pool—with me totally under water—I heard God say this to me: "That's the way I want you with me. Not part-way in; I want you *all* the way in to me!"

Shocked to hear God say this to me, I shot up out of the water and shouted to the heavens, "What do you *mean* you want me all the way in to you? I am *already* all the way in! I have given you my home, my medical practice, my family—everything." At that precise moment, I heard God speak to me for the second time, only this time more firmly: "I *said,* I don't want you *part*-way in. I want you *all* the way in to me." I had absolutely no idea what God meant, and I returned to my office quite perplexed.

The next morning I went to the operating room. The first surgery I had scheduled was to patch a hole in a man's eardrum. As I was scrubbing up, suddenly I heard God speak—not audibly, but within, more like a stream of thought. I heard, *You will never understand me and my ways concerning healing until you see me in the healing of this patient.*

As soon as the operation began, I understood what God was saying to me. I made an incision in the man's ear canal and elevated his eardrum. I then turned to the operating microscope and discovered that the tiny bones of the middle ear—the malleus, incus, and stapes—were engulfed with a white, cement-like material called tympanosclerosis. I tapped lightly on the bones and found they were frozen, making even the slightest movement impossible. Instantly, I knew that when I patched the hole in the man's eardrum, he would actually hear worse until I came back for a second operation to free up the ear bones (ossicles) and mobilize them. The reason this was true is that prior to the operation, sound could enter through the hole in the man's eardrum, bypass the ossicles, enter the round window (the "back door"), and stimulate the inner-ear hair cells that way. But the moment I sealed the hole in the eardrum, all the sound would be driven into the ossicles, and they could not move, as they were frozen in place. So, the man would have at least a 60-decibel hearing loss in that ear until I could return at a later date to mobilize his ear bones. I was trained to never do both steps at the same time. Doing that could introduce infection into the inner ear and cause a total loss of hearing. That day in the operating room, I said, "Lord, if this man hears better, then you are going to have to do it, because I know he will hear worse after this operation."

The next day, I was making rounds and it was time for my patient to go home. I wrote the usual prescriptions and gave him an appointment to see me in three weeks. Just as I was writing the discharge order in his chart, I suddenly felt a strong impression that I should pray for my patient. There was a nurse standing at my side, and I wasn't about to pray in front of her. Not only that, I had never prayed for a patient before and wasn't sure what I would say.

On the way back to the nursing station, the strong impression to pray for this man would not go away. So I grabbed a stethoscope on the pretense that I would listen to his chest before discharging him. I assumed the floor nurse would not return to the room a second time, but she did. Again, I shrugged off the impulse to pray, listened to the man's chest, gave the stethoscope to the nurse, and told God that at least I had tried. I completed rounds and was about to leave the hospital when again I received a strong urging to pray for my ear patient. This time I also heard God say, "I said I don't want you *part*-way in, I want you *all* the way in to me."

Being a man of great faith and courage, I ducked outside to the hospital fire escape, climbed down, and came to my patient's floor. His room was at the end of the hall, and I wouldn't have to walk past the nurse's station. I looked through the chicken-wire glass of the steel door, and seeing no nurse in sight, I darted into the man's room.

My patient was packing to go home and looked rather surprised to see me for the third time. I went straight to the point. "I know this may sound strange to you, but I believe I am supposed to pray for you before you go home." The man said, "Oh, praise God! My father is a pastor, and I would love for you to pray for me." Relieved, I placed my hands on the man's head, and instantly I knew how I was to pray. I said, "Lord, I pray for this man's ear and ask that the force that is binding his ear bones be removed, and that the bones in this man's ear will vibrate even as they did in his mother's womb." The prayer seemed strange to me, but the man said, "Praise God! Thank you, doctor."

Every day I wondered if I had done the right thing. Three weeks later my patient came back to the office for the scheduled appointment. When I called out his name, he said, "Dr. Graham, I can hear perfectly! My superior at work recognized it instantly and gave me a promotion." What the man didn't know was that normally at this point in the procedure, I would still have to remove the cotton ball from the patient's ear canal, suck out the ointment, and blow air into the eustachian tube before the patient would be able to hear. Furthermore, I knew that this man's ear bones were still frozen and immobile. I knew there could be no possibility of his hearing better without that second operation to mobilize his ear bones.

I removed the cotton ball and ointment, blew air up into his eustachian tube, and then sent the man into the soundproof room for a hearing test. My technician returned, beaming, and said, "Look, Dr. Graham, he can hear normal in that ear!" The man was shouting, "I told you so!"

I stared at the audiogram. There was no way this man could hear better after the operation I had performed—not without a second procedure. Yet, the test showed his hearing was now within the normal range!

For weeks I was elated but frustrated. God had healed a man, and I could not prove it to anyone. After all, I *did* operate on the man's ear. People would assume my operation had restored the man's hearing, but I knew better. I wondered why God hadn't had me just pray for the man and not operate on him. Then, it would be obvious that God had done a miracle. This way, it looked as if my surgery was responsible for the healing. I felt robbed. God didn't get the glory, and I couldn't prove that a miracle had taken place.

I struggled with this for weeks. Then one day, God said, "You will recall that I said you would never understand me and my ways concerning healing until you could see me in the healing of this man." Then I heard, "There will always be sufficient evidence to doubt if you want to doubt; there will always be sufficient evidence to believe if you want to believe."

I was shocked by the revelation and immediately understood that God was present in all healings, including those under the care of a physician. God had wanted me to know also that there would always be sufficient evidence to believe the healing was due to the doctor's skill, but there would also be sufficient evidence to believe that all healing is from God.

I understood too that I would never have come to this awareness had not God revealed it to me. That realization made me wonder how much I would miss if my heart was not always open to God. From that moment on, I began to pray, "Lord, I want to be *all* the way in to everything you have for me. I don't want to be just part-way in; I want to be totally submerged in you."

Chapter 4

Scrubbing a Few Pigs

Then Jesus said to the disciples, "There was a rich man who had a manager, and charges were brought to him that this man was squandering his property. So he summoned him and said to him, 'What is this that I hear about you? Give me an accounting of your management, because you cannot be my manager any longer.' Then the manager said to himself, 'What will I do, now that my master is taking the position away from me? I am not strong enough to dig, and I am ashamed to beg. I have decide what to do so that, when I am dismissed as manager, people may welcome me into their homes.' So, summoning his master's debtors one by one, he asked the first, 'How much do you owe my master?' He answered, 'A hundred jugs of olive oil.' He said to him, 'Take your bill, sit down quickly, and make it fifty.' Then he asked another, 'And how much do you owe?' He replied, 'A hundred containers of wheat.' He said to him, 'Take your bill and make it eighty.' And his master commended the dishonest manager because he had acted shrewdly; for the children of this age are more shrewd in dealing with their own generation than are the children of light. And I tell you, make friends for yourselves by means of dishonest wealth so that when it is gone, they may welcome you into the eternal homes. Whoever is faithful in very little is faithful also in much; and who-ever is dishonest in a very little is dishonest also in much. If then you have not been faithful with the dishonest wealth, who will entrust to you the true riches? And if you have not been faithful with what belongs to another, who will give you what is your own? No slave can serve two masters; for a slave will either hate the one and love the other, or be devoted to the one and despise the other. You cannot serve God and wealth." (Luke 16:1-13)

*J*esus' parable of the shrewd manager (who sometimes is referred to also as the unjust steward) is one of the hardest to understand. It is the story of a business manager who is accused of poor management, gets fired, and then begins manipulating accounts to feather his own nest. When his master learns what he has done, he commends the man. As if that isn't enough, Jesus tells his disciples to go and do likewise.

Confusing? You bet. So, what's going on? What is Jesus trying to say to us?

I believe it is significant that this parable follows the well-known parable of the prodigal son. There are similarities. At the outset, both men have squandered possessions. The dishonest manager has squandered his master's property, while the prodigal son has squandered his father's fortune in riotous living. After this, the two stories diverge. When the prodigal finds himself penniless, he goes to work doing manual labor in the fields and feeding swine. But when the steward finds himself penniless, he says, "I am not strong enough to dig, and I am too ashamed to beg." Slopping hogs was not for this man. The work was too hard.

I know all too well that slopping hogs can be hard work. As a boy I was once the proud owner of a large, red Duroc. At the time, my folks lived on a farm in the country and we had all kinds of animals, including pigs. One of the tasks my brothers and I had to do was to take care of a dozen or so hogs. We fed them, and, because we were trying to win a prize at the Louisiana State Fair, we scrubbed our pigs every day. So they'd look pretty. So we could win first prize and get a purple ribbon.

I cannot tell you how hard my brothers and I worked on those pigs. I was especially proud of my pig. She truly was beautiful, and I was proud to learn that red hogs were said to have been brought to this country by Columbus and de Soto. My Duroc was solid dark-red, almost mahogany in color. She was a large pig with a somewhat dish face and ears that drooped—proper features for her breed. Almost every week, the county agricultural agent would drop by just to look at my pig and tell me he thought I had the best-looking pig in the state. He loved her flat belly. It was a perfect straight line from front to back. Above all, he cautioned me not to overfeed my hog or she'd lose her lines.

Every night for months I fell asleep dreaming of winning first prize at the Louisiana State Fair. I could just see my pig and me pictured on the front page of our local newspaper, *The Shreveport Times*. That was no mere fantasy on my part. Every year around October when the fair came to town, the kid who won first prize was always seen on the front page holding a big check from some company like Kansas City Southern Railroad. The thought of winning that prize and getting my picture in the paper made me scrub my pig a little harder. I wanted her to be beautiful. I wanted to win that prize.

The shrewd manager in Luke 16 didn't want to work that hard. I guess his hands were too delicate for that kind of work. But he was desperate. Without employment he would soon be a social outcast and no one would welcome him into their home. And because he wasn't about to do manual labor, he turned to what had worked for him in the past: being resourceful, manipulating things for his own benefit, even if that meant he had to be downright dishonest.

In today's lingo, this guy was *streetwise*. He knew how to work the system. So, before turning in his ledger to the owner, he went to his clients and allowed them to lower the amount they owed. Of course, this made them very happy and ensured he would always be welcome in their homes, he would not be an outcast. His cleverness prompted the rich owner to commend his servant for being so shrewd.

When he finished telling the story, Jesus made an analogy. He told his disciples that just as this manager was shrewd in securing friends who would receive him in their earthly habitations, so too the people of God should be shrewd in spiritual matters—they should use their wealth and possessions wisely so they will be received into eternal habitations.

Fascinating. You can't take your money with you, but you can send it on ahead before you get there! And, how do you do that? You give your wealth to God's work, and Jesus says you will make friends for yourself in heaven.

Now, please understand that Jesus is not proclaiming that we can be saved by our good works. No, we are saved by God's grace and not by works. That's what the cross is all about. Jesus is addressing this message to men and women who are already his disciples—folks who are already children of light. What he is saying is that it is crucially important how the children of God use their possessions. In fact, according to Jesus, the issue is a matter of eternal significance. He is saying, if we are not faithful stewards with what we have on earth, we will never be faithful with the true riches of heaven. It's as if our time on earth is a testing ground to see whether or not we will be faithful in small things. If so, God will entrust us with big things.

Now I am sure most Christians would be shocked to learn this. Only, we shouldn't be surprised that the people of God don't know these things, when many ministers say they hate stewardship Sundays and don't like to preach about money and giving. Why *wouldn't* most Christians think stewardship is of little importance? If our spiritual leaders are too modest to talk about money, what can a person expect?

Yet, the fact is, Jesus wants you and me to see ourselves as stewards of God's possessions. Not owners, but stewards. This means we don't "possess" anything. Have you ever tried to possess something? The next thing you know, that which we try to possess possesses us. I once had a physician colleague who owned a weekend house in Arkansas. Every time he mentioned he was going up to Arkansas for the weekend, I envied him a bit and wished I had a place to escape to like he did. Then, one Friday morning in the surgeon's lounge, he said to me, "Every weekend when I go to Arkansas what I do is spend my entire weekend fixing up the place, and I return home totally exhausted. John, I don't own a weekend house; that house owns me!"

Indeed, our possessions can possess us. Besides, the truth is, everything we have—our talents, our gifts, and our possessions—everything is on loan from God; and we all know that which is loaned out must be returned to the rightful owner one day.

This means I am a steward—a manager—and nothing more. Everything I have belongs to God—always has, always will. I own nothing. None of us does. We just think we do. The fact is, we are merely stewards of that which God has given, and the bottom-line question of any steward is, "What are you doing with what you've got?"

This question leads me back to my pig story. For many months I scrubbed and fed that pig. She was beautiful, and I was so proud of her. Then one day my father came home and announced he had bought passage for the family to take a Caribbean cruise. We were all so excited that we packed up and left the farm in the hands of a caretaker. He was given instructions as to the feeding and care of all the animals, including my pig.

Eight days later I returned home, raced to the hog pen to see my championship pig, took one look at her, and thought I must have the wrong pig. A quick glance at the others, and I realized this was my pig. I almost fainted. She was caked in mud from snout to curly tail and looked like she never had been scrubbed, not once. But the worst thing of all was, her belly was no longer flat. Now, she had a pot-belly. Horrors! I couldn't believe it. All my months of hard work were gone in a single week.

The county agent showed up the next day. I told him I would work hard and would have my pig cleaned and trimmed up in time for the state fair. He just shook his head. "Son," he said, "you can scrub that pig all you want. You can make her look real pretty, but you'll never get that belly off her." He was right. For weeks I scrubbed and fed her meager portions, but she never got rid of her belly, and she didn't even place in the show.

I was devastated. I had given my pig into the management of a steward, and he had squandered my most prized possession. Worst of all, I felt I had betrayed myself. I had traded a purple ribbon and my picture in the paper for a week of fun in the sun. It was a painful lesson, and one I have never forgotten.

A final observation. I spent months scrubbing that pig just to win a prize that would soon pass away. Nothing eternal about it at all. I wonder: How many pigs am I scrubbing right now—seeking earthly prizes that will pass away?

Again and again, I need to take an accounting of my life and consider how I am spending my time, talents, and treasure. Only then can I make the adjustments required and quit scrubbing the "pigs" I continually accumulate in my life.

Chapter 5

Cupid's Bow and All

And he told them many things in parables, saying: "Listen! A sower went out to sow. And as he sowed, some seeds fell on the path, and the birds came and ate them up. Other seeds fell on rocky ground, where they did not have much soil, and they sprang up quickly, since they had no depth of soil. But when the sun rose, they were scorched; and since they had no root, they withered away. Other seeds fell among thorns, and the thorns grew up and choked them. Other seeds fell on good soil and brought forth grain, some a hundredfold, some sixty, some thirty. . . . Hear then the parable of the sower. When anyone hears the word of the kingdom and does not understand it, the evil one comes and snatches away what was sown in the heart; this is what was sown on the path. As for what was sown on rocky ground, this is the one who hears the word and immediately receives it with joy; yet such a person has no root, but endures only for a while, and when trouble or persecution arises on account of the word, that person immediately falls away. As for what was sown among thorns, this is the one who hears the word, but the cares of the world and the lure of wealth choke the word, and it yields nothing. But as for what was sown on good soil, this is the one who hears the word and understands it, who indeed bears fruit and yields, in one case a hundredfold, in another sixty, and in another thirty."

(Matthew 13:3-8; 18-23)

*P*art of my training as a plastic surgeon took place in Miami, Florida, under Dr. D. Ralph Millard Jr. During my stay in Miami, I heard Dr. Millard tell the story again and again about how he devised the technique that is used around the world for the repair of cleft lip— the procedure that would make him famous.

During the Korean Conflict, Ralph repaired a Korean child's cleft lip using the standard technique but was not happy with the result. Where the lip had been pulled together, it appeared tight—as if tissue were missing—and there was a vertical scar down the middle of the child's lip. He wanted an approach that would allow the person to grow up with a lip normal in appearance, cupid's bow and all. In his three-volume masterpiece entitled *Cleft Craft,* Millard tells the story of how he developed his new technique. [1]

To help study the problem, he had a photographer print a large picture of a child who had a cleft lip. Week after week he studied the picture, searching for a new technique, to no avail. All he could see was what had been done in the past. One evening he stayed up late studying the photographs until, exhausted, he fell asleep. Hours later he opened his eyes and while still lying on his side, glanced at the photographs that stood on an easel before him. Suddenly, Millard saw something he had never seen before. From that new perspective—lying on his side—he realized that all the normal parts of the upper lip were present, except that they were displaced and turned upwards. Surgical techniques had previously been designed in the belief that the center of the upper lip was absent. Ralph now realized this was not true. The normal tissue had been there all the time, but because it was in the wrong position, it went unrecognized.

Instantly, he understood why the traditional techniques could never produce a normal-appearing lip; typically, the normal tissue was discarded. Millard knew that what must be done is to keep the normal tissue, rotate it down into the proper position, advance the two edges, and suture them together. Returning normal tissue to its normal position would result in a normal lip, he concluded. Having devised his new approach, it was now time to put the theory into practice. Within hours, a little Korean boy became the first patient to have a Millard repair for a cleft lip. The result was all Millard had hoped for, and the child would go through life with a normal-appearing upper lip.

It would be hard to imagine Dr. Millard's excitement. He believed his new approach would revolutionize cleft lip surgery, and with great zeal he began to carry "the gospel" of his new technique to plastic sur-

---

1. D. Ralph Millard, Jr., *Cleft Craft: The Evolution of Its Surgery* (Boston: Little, Brown, 1976), Vol. 1, pp. 167-73.

gery meetings around the world. Only, these surgeons did not exactly embrace his new approach. In fact, some even turned up their noses and wouldn't listen.

Year after year, Millard worked to get his technique accepted by his colleagues. He saw his residents-in-training as "missionaries"—missionaries to carry the truth that he taught. In obvious parallels to the Scriptures, I often heard Dr. Millard tell us, "All I ask is for you to sow the seed—tell the message. Some seed will fall by the wayside, some will fall in rocky places, some will fall among thorns, but some will fall on good soil and bear fruit." One thing is certain—Ralph Millard believed his message would ultimately be accepted. Truth has a way of doing that, doesn't it?

In Matthew's Gospel, that is exactly what Jesus wanted to get across to his disciples. He wanted his disciples to know there would always be resistance to the message of God's kingdom. Jesus wanted his disciples to know that resistance doesn't mean they should stop sharing the message. No, like the sower who sows seed, we are to continue to spread the gospel message lavishly, everywhere, with every man, woman, and child, because we cannot discern who will receive it—some will and some won't. In due season, the gospel of Jesus Christ will bear fruit in the hearts and lives of many.

Our role is to be faithful in telling the story, and I believe we do that in our churches. Sunday after Sunday, in Word and in Sacrament, in preaching and in teaching, with every song we sing, through every Scripture we read, and with every Sunday school class we teach. Throughout the week, too—with every prayer we pray and every pastoral contact made. With warm smiles and phone calls to welcome visitors. With every underprivileged child we outfit for school, with every visit to the hospital, and with every Habitat for Humanity house we will build. With gifts to the people of other countries in their hour of great need, and with countless hours spent serving on the boards of charitable organizations around this great nation. Sunday after Sunday and week after week—in ways too numerous for me to name—Christians are sowing the seeds of God's love to everyone, everywhere. Yes, our role is to sow the seed, and the seed of God's Word will accomplish the purpose for which God has sent it.

In time, Ralph Millard was proved right. Eventually his approach came to be recognized around the world as the best way to repair a cleft lip. I am glad I was one of his residents, one of his "missionaries" sent out to spread the "gospel" message to those who would listen and to those who would not.

Yet, the gospel you and I have to share is far greater than that of any professor of plastic surgery. Ours is a message of good news that touches eternity and judgment itself. A message about the Word of God and four kinds of soil, only one of which will bear fruit. A message about Jesus, who is the divine Word Incarnate—a seed that is so fragile that you and I can reject it, if we choose. It is the message of God's love for all humankind. That message can be wasted, thrown away, trampled under-foot, crushed, and crucified. Yet, nothing can stop it. Reject it if you will; Scripture says that one day, every knee will bow and every tongue will confess that Jesus Christ is Lord. (See Isaiah 45:23; Romans 14:11.)

One day Dr. Millard looked at a little boy's picture from a new angle, and everything changed—a new way of seeing things burst into his heart. Like him, I have changed my perspective on many things, includ-ing this reading from Matthew's Gospel. I once thought this passage of Scripture was referring to four different kinds of people who had different kinds of hearts—that three out of four people would reject the gospel, and only those with "good" soil could receive God's Word. Then I came to realize there is another way to interpret this passage.

I now believe this passage can be interpreted to say that each of us can have all four of these soils. I know I always begin with a hard heart toward the next thing God wants to say to me. Usually, by the third time God says something to me, I begin to hear. Although my heart may be softer, it can still be a rocky place at best, or too shallow to retain what God has said. At other times my heart is full of "thorns," chocked with the cares of this world and focused on the deceitfulness of riches. At times there is no room at all for God in my life.

But, thanks be to God, we don't have to stay in any of these places. So, our heart is hardened, and our soul rocky? No problem. All we have to do is open our heart to God and God's will for our life. God can take hard-heartedness, all the thorny places in our lives, all that is out of position, and God can mold and shape us.

And the moment we give our lives to God, the Holy Spirit begins to work in our hearts and is never satisfied until we become like Christ. Yes, God keeps on working until our inner selves are made perfectly whole—"cupid's bow" and all.

Chapter 6

My Sky King Decoder Ring

Then I saw a new heaven and a new earth; for the first heaven and the first earth had passed away, and the sea was no more. And I saw the holy city, the new Jerusalem, coming down out of heaven from God, prepared as a bride adorned for her husband. And I heard a loud voice from the throne saying, "See, the home of God is among mortals. He will dwell with them; they will be his peoples, and God himself will be with them; he will wipe every tear from their eyes. Death will be no more; mourning and crying and pain will be no more, for the first things have passed away." And the one who was seated on the throne said, "See, I am making all things new." Also he said, "Write this, for these words are trustworthy and true." (Revelation 21:1-5)

I·f you are a person of a certain generation, then perhaps you, like me, ordered a Sky King decoder ring when you were a kid. *Sky King* was a radio program that offered prizes, a pre-television sales-marketing technique directed toward children. I was so excited the day I got my decoder ring. It had a dial you could turn and set in such a way as to unscramble what was an otherwise unreadable message. Immediately, I unscrambled several coded messages in the kit. I was thrilled. I was just a ten-year-old kid, but I could decipher a secretly coded message—something my parents could not do. What power!

Several years ago, I taught a Bible study on the book of Revelation. I think all of the participants would have enjoyed having a decoder ring to decipher Revelation's message. A few weeks after I began teaching the class, an amazing coincidence happened. While we were in the midst of our study of Revelation, religious group leader David Koresh was on TV proclaiming that God had given him the interpretation of the meaning of the seven seals, which he said were to be broken in the end time. As you may recall, a ninety-day standoff with the U.S.

government ended in the deaths of Koresh and about eighty of his Branch Davidian followers, men, women, and children, as armored tanks crushed through the walls of the group's Waco, Texas, compound, creating a flaming inferno. Two years later—to the very day—a rental truck exploded in front of the Alfred P. Murrah Federal Building in Oklahoma City, killing 169 innocent people in a retaliatory protest over the earlier event.

Apocalypse, now. These are the times in which we live. These are the times in which we must raise our children. Shortly after the explosion in Oklahoma City, a friend of mine was teaching children's chapel. When he asked if the children had any questions, indeed they did. Questions like these: "Will a bomb go off in our city?" "Will we be killed like the children in Oklahoma?" "Can you still go to heaven if you don't have a body?" That last question was a good one. When the mournful sixteen-day search ended, 167 had been removed from the rubble, including nineteen children. Two more were known dead, but their bodies could not be found. A child asked me, "Can you go to heaven without a body?"

When death hangs like a shroud, we must address our fears and the fears of our children. And when we need an eternal perspective on things, no book of the Bible provides it as well as Revelation. The word *revelation* means to make manifest, to uncover, to reveal secrets. Although many would see Revelation as a book shrouded in mystery and impossible to understand, the author, John, intends his book to reveal the hidden things of God and to bring comfort to the people in their day-to-day struggles in life.

Without doubt, John used highly symbolic language, and to understand symbolic language we need to know the code to interpret the correct meaning of its message. I'd like to suggest that similar to my Sky King decoder ring, we need a Revelation decoder. Only, don't expect the decoder to give just one interpretation of Revelation. The fact is, you can set your decoder on several images, and with each image you will get a different interpretation of Revelation.

First, you can set your ring on the image of King David, the mighty warrior. Many in the first century thought that was how they'd recognize the Messiah. They believed the Messiah would be a man of war who would free the people of Israel from bondage to Rome. Set your decoder on the image of King David the warrior, and you will interpret

Revelation as a picture of an end-time war in which the forces of good achieve a military victory over the forces of evil. Think like that, and you may begin to stash away weapons in your basement. Or perhaps you will bury them in your backyard flower bed until you hear some end-time messiah's battle cry. Ultimately, you'll likely make plans to dig up your weapons and kill all the enemies of God. But there's one problem: How can you tell which people are God's enemies?

A second image on the decoder ring is that of Caesar, who created a worldwide empire. Set your decoder on the picture of Caesar, and you can interpret Revelation through the eyes of a one-world government where a great world leader will bring order out of chaos. Think like that, and you will keep your eyes open for a man or woman to arise who has a special charisma, an unusually gifted leader. Only one problem: You could be mistaken and led astray. So, you had better have a critical eye to discern impostors. The news media do a good job of bringing down those in authority. Only, no one is left standing. We are left without leadership and with no heroes.

A third image is that of King Solomon, a man of enormous wealth and power. Set your decoder on King Solomon, and you will interpret Revelation as saying that God blesses those who have wealth and power, as these will take over the earth. Think like that and you will be driven to acquire as much wealth and power as you can, and you will strive to be with those who do. Better be sure to keep your wealth and power to yourself. Don't give anything to others, because if you give it away, you will lose your power, won't you?

There is yet another image on the Revelation decoder ring. It's not the image of a warrior, a politician, or one with wealth and power. This image is not that of a man at all. It is the image of a lamb. One who could do no warfare. One who could not persuade the masses. One who could not acquire great wealth or power. This lamb appears slain—one who has no visible power. This gentle Lamb is Jesus Christ.

Seen through the eyes of the Lamb, Revelation can only be interpreted as an act of God's redeeming love. That is the message of all of Scripture: God is reaching out to redeem people. We see this with Noah, where one family was redeemed. We see it with Moses, where one nation was redeemed. And what the Lamb is saying to us in Revelation is that in the end times, God will redeem all humankind—people of every nation and kindred. Not just people—God will redeem and restore creation as well. Then, there will be a new heaven and a new earth.

The Revelation decoder applies to every relationship in life as well, including Waco and the Branch Davidians. David Koresh set his decoder on the image of King David, the warrior. As a result, he saw people as either lining up on the side of God or on the side of Satan. He believed those who accepted his private interpretation of Scripture were on the side of God and everyone else was on the side of the enemy. Believing Revelation described a final war between good and evil, his followers stockpiled weapons. They needed to slay God's enemies, or so they reasoned.

Of course, stockpiling weapons eventually caught the attention of the federal government, whose decoder is set on the image of Caesar, the politician. They want the people who elected them to believe they are able to solve any problem. So, the Bureau of Alcohol, Tobacco, and Firearms surrounded the Branch Davidians, and what followed was a ninety-day standoff.

Next, the national television news media arrived with their decoder turned to the image of King Solomon—wealth and power. Day after day the reporters declared, "This standoff is costing millions of taxpayer dollars every day. The meter is running." Again and again reporters asked, "How long will the Bureau wait before they do something?"

Do something they did. Who can ever forget the scene of tanks crushing through the walls of the compound? Who can ever forget the tower of flames? Who can forget that many people died, including innocent children?

Exactly two years later, on April 19, 1995, there was the awful explosion in Oklahoma City that destroyed the lives of 169 men, women, and children. Who can ever forget the picture of the fireman carrying the ashes-covered body of a little girl from the rubble? Who can ever forget the mothers' wailing cries as one by one, they learned that their children had been killed, crushed under a mountain of concrete and steel? Who can ever forget Edye Smith, the young mother—daughter of missionaries—who sat with a framed picture of her two dead boys under one arm and her sons' two teddy bears under the other? Two days later we learned that two men had rendered an eye-for-eye retribution for the Waco massacre. The government had destroyed the Branch Davidian compound, so they in turn destroyed a government building. King David warriors on both sides were fighting for what they believed to be right. All the while, innocent people suffered and were slain.

Finally, mercifully, someone turned the Revelation decoder to the image of the Lamb, and people across this nation began to reach out to rescue those who were buried under the mountain of concrete and steel. Men and women came from everywhere. Food, supplies, and sophisticated electronic sensing devices were sent in the hope that many could be rescued. Sadly, only a few were found alive.

On the Sunday afternoon following the bombing, there was a gigantic prayer meeting held in Oklahoma City. Speaker after speaker, including the mayor, the governor, and the President of the United States stood to encourage the devastated people of a ravaged city. What did these men and women offer to encourage the citizens of Oklahoma City? One after another, they pointed to God and the strength that only God can give.

A rabbi recalled a litany of cities that had been destroyed over the history of humankind. Cities like Sodom and Gomorrah, Jericho, and Babylon—cities destroyed and never rebuilt. Then, he reminded everyone of Jerusalem, the city that had been reduced to rubble and yet was rebuilt by men and women of faith, hope, and courage. He said that though many had died in the bombing, like Jerusalem, Oklahoma City would be rebuilt too.

The meeting ended with a message by the evangelist Billy Graham. He quoted Revelation 21:1-5 and helped the people catch a glimpse of eternity when he said, "Today the heavens have opened for these innocent children. They are now with God where they shall neither hunger nor thirst anymore, and God shall wipe away every tear."

When we stand in the face of death and destruction such as that of Oklahoma City and realize that at any moment we too could vanish from the face of this earth, I am glad that we have sacred Scriptures that tell us of the promise of eternal life. Revelation provides a vision of people from every tribe and nation on earth, millions upon millions of people, who will one day stand before the throne of God.

What can we tell our children? We cannot promise that bad things won't happen to them. The fact is that we will all suffer and we will all die. What we *can* do is keep our Revelation decoder turned to the image of the Lamb and remember that to be human means we are more than just flesh and blood, here one day and gone the next. We are created in the image of God, and because we have been united with Jesus Christ in his death, burial, and resurrection, we belong to God and will never perish. No one can take us out of God's hand. No one. A bomb may kill our body, but a bomb can never take us away from God! When we die—at whatever age that might be, young or old—when we die, we will be where God is, forever and ever. In the meantime, we rejoice in his promise that he will never leave us or forsake us, no matter what we may endure. That's what we can tell our children and our grandchildren. Also, be sure to tell them to set their decoder on the right image.

Imagine what it would be like if everyone had his or her decoder set on the image of the Lamb. Then God's will *would* be done on earth as in heaven.

Chapter 7

The Most "Importantest" Thing of All

"If another member of the church sins against you, go and point out the fault when the two of you are alone. If the member listens to you, you have regained that one. But if you are not listened to, take one or two others with you, so that every word may be confirmed by the evidence of two or three witnesses. If the member refuses to listen to them, tell it to the church; and if the offender refuses to listen even to the church, let such a one be to you as a Gentile and a tax collector. Truly I tell you, whatever you bind on earth will be bound in heaven, and whatever you loose on earth will be loosed in heaven. Again, truly I tell you, if two of you agree on earth about anything you ask, it will be done for you by my Father in heaven. For where two or three are gathered in my name, I am there among them." (Matthew 18:15-20)

What parent doesn't love to ask his or her children what they learned in school that day? Our daughter, Ginger, asked her four-year-old son, Steven, this question on his first day in preschool, and he said, "The most importantest thing we learned today is how to be ladies and gentlemen." I'm glad our schools are teaching our children how to be ladies and gentlemen. I suspect this may be the most "importantest" thing for adults to learn as well.

Most of us would say harmony is one of our core values. Nevertheless, conflict is a part of life. If you talk to almost anyone long enough, you will soon discover you are committed to a different set of values and priorities in life. And because we have so much invested in these choices, we experience conflict—at church, at work, and at home. All this comes as no surprise to anyone who is married, or anyone who has had parents for that matter.

I had never seen my mother and father have a disagreement until I was awakened one night to hear heated words being exchanged by them. Then my dad screamed at my mother, "Don't shout—the boys will hear you!" Too late, this boy had already heard. Walls aren't thick enough to shield a child from a midnight argument, and walls aren't thick enough to shield a church from conflict, either. That is precisely why Jesus taught his disciples how we are to deal with conflict when we experience it.

Jesus said that when we experience conflict, the first thing we should do is take responsibility in the matter and seek to be reconciled with the person who has offended us. Most of us avoid the problematic person, thinking that if we steer clear, maybe the problem will go away. The dynamic at work is fear, and fear paralyzes, so we do nothing. Yet, more often than not, unresolved conflict only escalates with time.

The responsibility for solving the conflict between my mother and father belonged to my parents. And the same is true for each of us. When a conflict arises in our household, with a friend or coworker, or in church—Jesus is quite clear—we are first to go to that person, share our concerns, and seek reconciliation. If this does not succeed, we are to take another person. If that doesn't work, we are to submit the matter to those in leadership and abide by their decision. Whatever the leaders bind, let it be bound, and whatever they loose, let it be loosed. Forgive the other person and move on with life. In the church, reconciling our differences is essential if our love is to be genuine. Otherwise, all we do in the name of God is a sham.

This is the pattern that Jesus taught for dealing with conflict. But we don't learn that lesson. Instead, we learn how to deal with conflict early in life at home—from our parents and our siblings. Later, we are taught the art of conflict management on the school ground—from our peers. For the most part, what we are taught is dysfunctional behavior, at best.

So, later in life when conflict comes, instead of seeking reconciliation with the one who has offended us, we go to someone else—usually a parent or friend—and tell them our side of the story. What does a parent or friend do? They often use the occasion to draw closer to us by telling us we did the right thing. In commenting on your marital strife, a friend may say, "I wouldn't put up with that for one minute. Kick the louse out!" Your friend has strengthened the relationship with you, but at the expense of your marriage.

Psychologists have a term for this. It is called *triangulation*. We triangulate when we talk about someone who is not present. Of course, we talk about other people all the time—that's to be expected—but we "triangulate" when we undermine someone who is not present. Children often triangulate one parent against the other.

It is easy to be drawn into triangulating conversation. Pastoral counselors are taught not to do that. Instead of talking about someone who is not present, they will ask the persons to talk about themselves—tell how they feel. In marital conflict, a counselor will encourage the person to go back to his or her spouse and seek to be reconciled. The goal is to restore the marriage, not build a relationship with the one who came for counseling. The only exception might be where violence is involved.

You don't have to be a professional counselor to use this approach. All of us can listen attentively and affirm the person's pain without sacrificing the person who is not present. We can encourage our friend to take responsibility, to go to the other person, and to seek reconciliation. We can suggest that our friend and the other person go see a pastor or professional counselor together. One more thing, we can always pray with our friend, a simple prayer, in our own words: "Lord, I know you love Mary, and that you love John, too. I pray that you will heal their pain and restore their relationship. I ask this in your name. Amen."

What has happened? First of all, we supported our friend, and, by remaining neutral, we helped defuse the situation. We encouraged our friend to take personal responsibility for bringing the conflict to resolution. This empowered her so that she does not feel helpless. And by praying for them both, we have brought God into the equation and have been an instrument to help restore unity between two people who are loved by God.

Someone may say, "But what if you cannot resolve a conflict? What if the other person won't talk? What if nothing works?" Jesus said we are to pray for our enemies and for those who despitefully use us. We are to love them and not try to seek revenge. Instead, we are to walk humbly, ask for forgiveness when we need to, and remember the apostle Paul's admonition, "'If your enemies are hungry, feed them; if they are thirsty, give them something to drink. . . . ' Do not be overcome by evil, but overcome evil with good" (Romans 12:20-21).

That is Christ's way—overcoming evil with good—and I don't know anyone who needs to learn this more than the people of God. We seem to think that conflict should never happen to us—so we pretend it isn't happening. Yet, the church wrestled for hundreds of years before coming to the wording of the Nicene Creed. Why then should we be surprised when churches have conflict over such emotionally charged issues as human sexuality?

Many seem to think that not saying anything controversial will make for unity. But that is not true. Holding a belief and not sharing it does not mean we are in agreement. True unity comes about when we have the freedom to share our concerns, experience conflict, and still have the grace to be reconciled one to another.

The Bible begins with the story of the Garden of Eden, when humankind said we didn't need God any longer. Amazingly, we rejected God but God did not reject us. Instead, day after day, God continues to tell us that he loves us and wants to restore our relationship. When we wouldn't listen, God sent the prophets to call us back to God. Christians believe that God sent his own son, Jesus, to live among us, and in his death to show us that the way of life is the way of the cross. In 2 Corinthians 5:19-21, Paul says that we have been given the ministry of reconciliation—the ministry of pointing people who are far from God toward God, and the ministry of pointing people who are in conflict back to one another.

The more I think about it, the more I know little four-year-old Steven was right when he said, "The most importantest thing of all is that we learn how to be ladies and gentlemen." It is true for preschool children, and it is true for adults as well.

It's all about reconciliation, and reconciliation has been God's way of dealing with conflict ever since humankind decided we wanted a divorce from God.

Chapter 8

Forrest Gump—Labeled and Discarded

Now when Jesus came into the district of Caesarea Philippi, he asked his disciples, "Who do people say that the Son of Man is?" And they said, "Some say John the Baptist, but others Elijah, and still others Jeremiah or one of the prophets." He said to them, "But who do you say that I am?" Simon Peter answered, "You are the Messiah, the Son of the living God." And Jesus answered him, "Blessed are you, Simon son of Jonah! For flesh and blood has not revealed this to you, but my Father in heaven."

(Matthew 16:13-17)

*I*n the movie *Forrest Gump,* every time someone tried to pin the label "stupid" on Forrest, he would say, "My mother always said, 'Stupid is as stupid does.'" Like Forrest, I too have had a number of labels applied to me. Perhaps you carry a few yourself.

As a boy, I had enough blonde, curly hair to be called "Cotton Top" or "Cotton," for short. And when I sat next to my two brothers, they called the three of us "Cotton Patch." That was enough to make me never want to sit next to my brothers. Most often I was called "Shorty." I was so short that no one wanted me on his or her baseball team— when they chose up sides, I was always left out. Once my mother said that our family doctor was tall, dark, and handsome. I thought, "He is tall, dark, and handsome, and I am short, blonde, and ugly." Those were my labels.

Another person who experienced this type of labeling was a woman who wrote about her experience in an article for the Shreveport magazine *Up River.* She wrote, "I vividly remember that rainy day in April of 1991 when Shreveport experienced debilitating floods. The day those floods came was the day my husband and I separated. It was the day my ten-month-old son took his first step. It was the day I became a single mom." As if this didn't make life tough enough, she told of the day she opened a local society magazine to find her name in a column featuring single men and women. "The first sentence summed up my life in one short phrase, 'divorced with one child.' What a definition! It was like a Scarlet letter D that would forever brand me a divorcée." There is a powerful scene in *Forrest Gump* in which Forrest's best friend, Jenny Curran, returns to the house where she had been abused early in life. In fury she begins throwing rocks at the dilapidated structure. Finally, in exhaustion, she falls to the ground. Forrest expresses what she is feeling: "Sometimes there just aren't enough rocks to throw."

I suspect we all know what Forrest is talking about. We can recall those times in our own lives when there just aren't enough rocks to throw. Many know the trauma of divorce and bear the label "divorcée" or "divorcé." Others, after giving their best years on the job, were termed "deadwood" and released, forced then into bearing the label "unemployed." Others know what it means to carry the label "bankrupt," "failure," "addict," "controller," or "workaholic." One way or another, as a consequence of human sin, every person has been labeled something or other.

Jesus knew what it meant to be labeled. The Pharisees called Jesus a friend of sinners, a glutton, and a wine-bibber. On another occasion, Jesus was said to be demon-possessed. His own family labeled him as insane (see Mark 3:21). Because he cast out evil spirits, many called him Beelzebul—the king of evil spirits. So, Jesus was taking a risk when he asked his disciples, "Who do people say that I am?" His disciples could have reminded him of the labels I have just mentioned. Instead, they answered with some other labels. "Some say you are John the Baptist; others, Elijah; and still others, one of the prophets."

What did they mean by this? Were they saying Jesus was a reincarnation of a prophet of old, or Elijah, or John the Baptist? I don't think so. For many people, Jesus fit the category of John the Baptist—one who called people to repentance. To others Jesus was like the prophets of old—even Elijah, the greatest prophet of all. Elijah, who commanded the rain to cease and it ceased for three years (see James 5:17). Elijah, who had the power to stretch himself out over a widow's dead son and raise the boy from the dead (see 1 Kings 17:8-24). Elijah, who went up to heaven in a fiery chariot (see 2 Kings 2:1-11). To many, Jesus fit that imagery.

While labels help us define and communicate our understanding, they also limit our vision of other people. And labeling folks is one way we gain power over them, because if I label you, I de-personalize you, and if I do that, I can dismiss you. That, I believe, is why Jesus was not flattered by even such glorious labels as saying he was a prophet, or Elijah, or John the Baptist. These labels meant the people did not see him as the unique person he was.

Jesus asked a second question. This one was directed to his own disciples: "But, who do you say that I am?" The question must have caused a deafening silence to fall over the Twelve. They were puzzled. Why wasn't Jesus satisfied with their answer? What Jew wouldn't want to be included with the likes of Elijah the prophet? Jesus pressed them to go beyond labels, beyond the categories that provided only a limited understanding of his nature. Finally, Peter broke the silence and said, "You are the Messiah."

All three of the Synoptic Gospels—Matthew, Mark, and Luke—tell of Peter's confession, and each story sheds a little more light on what took place. In Mark's Gospel Peter said, "You are the Messiah" (8:29). *Christ* is the Greek word for *Messiah,* which means "the anointed one." In the Gospel of Luke, Peter takes it one step further, referring to Jesus as "the Messiah of God" (9:20). And in Matthew's Gospel Peter responds to Jesus, "You are the Messiah, the Son of the living God" (16:15-16).

Taking all three Gospels together, we have this description. Jesus is: The Messiah. The Christ. The Anointed One. The Son of God. Now, that's an image that breaks the boundaries of all previous categories and goes beyond all other labels. Peter was saying that Jesus was not just one among many prophets; to Peter, Jesus was the One about whom all the prophets had prophesied. Just as labels limit our understanding of Jesus Christ, so too our labels limit our appreciation of the people we live with every day of our lives. Let me give you an example. I have heard the rector of a particular church identified as a great manager. I have also heard that same rector labeled unfavorably as "a CEO, corporate-style pastor." Recognize the difference?

I believe we should make a distinction between a description and a label. A description is meant to enlarge our understanding of someone. We say someone is "single" or "married." And we describe some as being "young adults," some as "elderly," and some as "physically challenged." This is all a necessary part of communication. But when we label a person, we focus on one narrow aspect of that individual and define him or her with that judgment. In doing so, we ignore the person's totality. That is why labels can be so vicious—they are too narrow, too pejorative, and provide only a limited, single-focused view of that person.

Over the years, I have gotten to know the rector I mentioned above. I would agree he is a good manager. But because I have come to know him personally, I also know he is far more than a "CEO, corporate-style manager." I wouldn't even describe him that way, because I have seen tears stream from his eyes when I showed him that moving article in Shreveport's *Up River* magazine. He has a pastor's heart and embraces people in need. I also found him to be a man of God—one who gets before God and can hear God's voice. For all these reasons, I refuse to label and pigeonhole him. I cannot just say he is a CEO-style rector and dismiss him. If I do that, I miss the full potential of this great leader whom God has placed in the church.

And, if I can't do that with this rector, neither can I do that with anyone. The fact is, everyone is far more wonderful than all the labels I could use. Each person is a gift from God. Each is to be valued and held as precious by all.

We don't use labels just for individuals. Labels also have the potential to divide groups of people and separate folks into camps. In Israel, we have Palestinians and Jews. In Ireland, there are said to be Protestants and Catholics. This has meant that many citizens within one's own country are seen as enemies, and thus the countless civil wars throughout human history. Nor is labeling limited to broad categories such as Catholics and Protestants. Protestant Christians are said to be Evangelical, Fundamentalist, Conservative, Liberal, or Charismatic. Yet, no human being is any one of these labels, and we need to remember that.

Anglicans love to talk about the *via media,* "the middle way," which doesn't mean we straddle fences on issues. In its best sense, the *via media* means we seek to embrace all points of view simultaneously. It refers to an inclusiveness that keeps the dialogue open. It means listening because each position has something to say that we need to hear. The best way I can describe the *via media* is to say it means holding one extreme position in one hand and the other position in the other—

holding both positions in a tension of love. When at our best, we Anglicans practice this and will not allow ourselves to use labels to discard people. Rather, we use these terms to incorporate and to affirm.

Every now and then someone will say, "I hear you have Evangelicals attending your church." I respond, "Yes, we do, and we are happy, because we want to share the glorious gospel of Jesus Christ with everyone. Evangelicals have much to say to us." I also respond, "Yes, we have Fundamentalists in our church—for we are indeed men and women to whom the Word of God is precious." I also say, "Yes, we have Conservatives—for we are people who hold and value the traditions of our Anglican heritage." And, "Yes, we have Liberals in this place—for we are people sensitive to the needs of others and desire to have a powerful outreach to the disadvantaged in our city." "Yes, we have Charismatics, for we earnestly desire to see the Holy Spirit alive and present in our midst." I'll also say to anyone, "Yes, we have skeptics in our church—individuals who have doubts but are men and women of faith struggling to believe, and we respect their struggle."

Divergent points of view are present in the church and always have been. We would not want it any other way—for the message of Jesus Christ is far too wonderful to be encompassed by any one of these expressions alone. Paul said that in his efforts to spread the gospel, he had become "all things to all people" (1 Corinthians 9:22). We also want to be all things to all people, because we truly want to open our hearts to all whom God sends our way—whatever "labels" they may bear.

Forrest Gump was called stupid, but he did many wise things, while those who thought they were smart did stupid things and messed up their lives. To "natural" eyes, the cross of Jesus Christ may appear stupid and meaningless. Many would label the cross a sign of failure; but in God's eyes, the cross represents the wisdom of the universe, the plan of God from the very foundation of the earth. Seen with spiritual eyes, the cross is a message of profound love—a love so great it can only be expressed by God's Son coming to earth as a human being, living and dying for us.

Here, "Stupid is as stupid does" takes on eternal significance.

Chapter 9

Too Numb to Feel

On the way to Jerusalem Jesus was going through the region between Samaria and Galilee. As he entered a village, ten lepers approached him. Keeping their distance, they called out, saying, "Jesus, Master, have mercy on us!" When he saw them, he said to them, "Go and show yourselves to the priests." And as they went, they were made clean. Then one of them, when he saw that he was healed, turned back, praising God with a loud voice. He prostrated himself at Jesus' feet and thanked him. And he was a Samaritan. Then Jesus asked, "Were not ten made clean? But the other nine, where are they? Was none of them found to return and give praise to God except this foreigner?" Then he said to him, "Get up and go on your way; your faith has made you well."

(Luke 17:11-19)

*I*n 1994, I was the preacher at an ecumenical Thanksgiving Day worship service. It was held at Wheeler Avenue Baptist Church, a predominantly African American church in Houston. I was thrilled to be asked to preach in the service and spent several weeks prayerfully searching for the right passage in Scripture. I finally settled on the story of the ten lepers who were healed but only one returned to give thanks for his healing. Thinking about lepers and leprosy, my thoughts immediately went to a fellow surgeon, Dr. Paul Brand.

Dr. Brand dedicated his entire life to caring for patients afflicted with leprosy. He has written a powerful and moving book entitled *Fearfully and Wonderfully Made*. Read a portion of his account:

As a boy growing up in India, I idolized my missionary father who responded to every human need he encountered. Only once did I see him hesitate to give help. It happened when I was seven years old. Three strange men trudged up the dirt path to our home. At first glance they seemed like hundreds of others who streamed to our home for medical treatment.

But as they approached I noticed something different about these men: they had a mottled quality to their skin, thick, swollen foreheads and ears, and strips of blood-stained cloth bandaged their feet. As they came closer, I noticed all three lacked portions of their fingers and one had no toes.

My mother's reaction differed from her usual gracious hospitality. Her face turned pale and she became tense. "Run and get Papa," she said. "Take your sister, and both of you stay in the house." My sister obeyed, but after calling my father I scrambled to a vantage point. Something sinister was happening, and I didn't want to miss it. My heart pounded violently as I saw the same look of uncertainty, almost fear, pass across my father's face. He stood nervously, awkwardly, as if he didn't know what to do. I had never seen my father like that.

Finally in a weak voice he said, "There is not much we can do. I'm sorry." Then, seeing their obvious disappointment, he said, "wait where you are; don't move. I'll do what I can." He ran to the dispensary and soon returned with a roll of bandages, a can of salve, and a pair of surgical gloves he struggled to put on. This was most unusual—I had never seen my father wear surgeon's gloves to examine anyone else.

Father washed the strangers' feet, applied ointment to their sores, and bandaged them. Strangely, they did not wince or cry out as he touched their open wounds. While Father bandaged the men, Mother had been arranging a selection of fruit in a wicker basket. She set it on the ground beside them and suggested they take the basket. They took the fruit but left the basket, and as they disappeared over the ridge I went to pick it up.

"No!" Mother insisted. "Don't touch it! And don't go near that place where they sat." Silently, I watched my father take the basket and burn it, then wash his hands with hot water and soap. Then mother bathed my sister and me, though we had no direct contact with the visitors.

That incident was my first exposure to leprosy, the oldest recorded disease and the most dreaded throughout human history.[1]

It is hard for us in the twenty-first century to imagine what life would have been like in the first century for someone with leprosy. Today the disease is treatable, almost extinct. But for these ten lepers in Luke 17, life meant that they had to live with a horribly deforming and disfiguring illness that affected every area of their life.

---

1. Paul Brand and Philip Yancey, *Fearfully and Wonderfully Made* (Grand Rapids, Mich.: Zondervan, 1980), pp. 35-37.

In medical school we studied this disease. Textbooks called it Hansen's disease, but every student knew it as leprosy. In pathology class we looked at the organism under the microscope and studied the effects of the disease upon the human body. Leprosy attacks the sensory nerves of the body—the nerves that provide the sense of feeling. Most of us take the gift of touch for granted. We hardly think about it. Yet it is an incredibly important function. In one sense, the ability to touch and feel is part of what makes us human.

The sensory nerve endings in the tips of our fingers are remarkable. Normally, a person can sweep a hand across a glass surface and distinguish between one that is perfectly smooth and one etched with lines a mere 1/2000th of an inch deep. It is this keen sense of touch that allows the person who is blind to read books written in Braille.

Not only that, but when we are asleep, touch is the most alert of our senses. Some people won't budge a muscle if they are asleep, even if you yell loudly at them. You can turn on the lights or open the blinds, and they will hardly notice. These folks buy those horrible alarm clocks that have a tooth-jarring, clanging sound that can be heard three blocks away. They can sleep right through it. But the slightest touch to the body, and most will instantly awake. Touch is the sense that invigorates and awakens.

We also use touch to communicate our love for another person, and in this way the sense of touch can reach to our deepest emotions. Consider a beloved friend who holds your hand when you are gravely ill and near the point of death. Imagine the gentle touch of the one you love, a tender caress and warm embrace. Think about cuddling a baby's soft cheek against yours.

The sense of touch arouses and awakens. It warms our heart as well.

The patient with leprosy loses all of this because the nerves that supply the sense of touch have been damaged. Gradually the person with leprosy becomes trapped in a body that cannot feel, and because others dread the disease, he or she is forced to live in isolation, away from the rest of society, outside the city gate.

Most of us avoid pain and think that we don't need it. This is not true. Pain is actually an important protection mechanism God has given us. Pain is a red flag waving to tell us, "Better do something, you are about to be hurt!" Put our finger in the fire and we jerk it back. Otherwise, we would be severely burned.

We all know what it means to be hurt emotionally, to have pain that grieves the heart. That too is a protective mechanism. Hurt us emotionally, and God has designed us to withdraw to a safe place. One of the most important things parents can teach their children is to honor their feelings. If they feel something is wrong, if they are hurt or frightened, your children need to know it is okay to get up, leave, and come home. It has been said that home is the place where we feel safe. Wherever we can be ourselves and relax is home. Yet, for many, home is no longer a safe place. Home is where you can be abused, assaulted, and violated. Physically and emotionally abused folk may have to leave home in order to find "home."

Some have been so hurt they can no longer feel anything—they are numb. It is dangerous to be numb, because one who is numb is no longer able to recognize when he or she is being hurt. A numb person goes through life making all the motions, but nothing touches them, their hope is gone, and suicide is but a step away.

All this and more happened to the ten men in Luke 17. They had lost the ability to touch physically, and they had been abused by society to the point they were numb on the inside as well. All the joy of life was gone for these men. They wore burlap bags for clothes and shouted a warning to everyone they met, "Unclean! Unclean! Save yourself, run the other way! A leper is approaching!"

Scripture says that ten men with leprosy approached Jesus. Ten! Enough to send shivers up and down the spine of any citizen of the first century. Standing "afar off," they saw Jesus, lifted their voices, and began to cry out—only they didn't cry, "Unclean! Unclean!" Instead, they shouted, "Master, have mercy on us!" What a difference a few words can make. These men saw in Jesus a person who had compassion for them, and they saw in Jesus a person who was not afraid of them.

Jesus said, "Go and show yourselves to the priests." They obeyed, which was an act of faith on their part, and as they went they were cleansed and healed. But one of them, when he "saw" that he was healed, returned, and with a loud voice glorified God. Of course he rejoiced. He had lived for years with that horrible disease, and now he was cleansed. Now he could feel again! Now he could return to society. Live with people. *Touch* people. Put his cheek against a baby's cheek. Feel the tears of joy coursing down his cheeks. So this man returned with joy in his heart to thank God and to thank Jesus.

Scripture says that one man "saw" he was healed. What a fascinating observation. Surely all ten saw that they were healed. Yet, Scripture says only one man really saw. The others were healed, but they didn't see—not really, not with spiritual eyes. Only one man truly "saw"; and when he came to "see" that it was God who had healed him, the man returned, praised God in a loud voice, threw himself at Jesus' feet, and thanked him, again and again.

God knows when we are hurting. God also knows when we have been hurt so much that we are numb and can feel nothing. And God wants us to be healed and to be able to feel again. Many people think the pain they suffer is because God is displeased with them. That is not true. God loves everyone, including those who are sick and in pain. Jesus said he came that we might have life and have it more abundantly (see John 10:10). God wants to wipe away every tear, so that we might sorrow no more (Revelation 21:4).

Matthew's Gospel tells the story of a man with leprosy who cried out to Jesus and said, "Lord, if you choose, you can make me clean." To this man Jesus said, "I do choose. Be made clean!" And "immediately his leprosy was cleansed" (Matthew 8:2-3).

Dr. Paul Brand spent his entire life as a surgeon taking care of those afflicted with Hansen's disease. He developed new surgical procedures, tendon transfers, to restore function to the hands of his patients. He fashioned shoes so they would not injure their feet. Brand was a man who followed in the footsteps of the Great Physician, Jesus. May we also follow in his footsteps and do all in our power to bring healing to the pain of others, especially those who have been hurt so badly that they are numb and feel pain no more.

Chapter 10

Cast Away and Advent

In those days Mary set out and went with haste to a Judean town in the hill country, where she entered the house of Zechariah and greeted Elizabeth. When Elizabeth heard Mary's greeting, the child leaped in her womb. And Elizabeth was filled with the Holy Spirit and exclaimed with a loud cry, "Blessed are you among women, and blessed is the fruit of your womb. And why has this happened to me, that the mother of my Lord comes to me? For as soon as I heard the sound of your greeting, the child in my womb leaped for joy. And blessed is she who believed that there would be a fulfillment of what was spoken to her by the Lord." And Mary said, "My soul magnifies the Lord, and my spirit rejoices in God my Savior, for he has looked with favor on the lowliness of his servant. Surely, from now on all generations will call me blessed; for the Mighty One has done great things for me, and holy is his name. His mercy is for those who fear him from generation to generation. He has shown strength with his arm; he has scattered the proud in the thoughts of their hearts. He has brought down the powerful from their thrones, and lifted up the lowly; he has filled the hungry with good things, and sent the rich away empty. He has helped his servant Israel, in remembrance of his mercy, according to the promise he made to our ancestors, to Abraham and to his descendants forever." And Mary remained with her about three months and then returned to her home. (Luke 1:39-56)

*O*ccasionally on the church's liturgical calendar, the fourth Sunday of Advent falls on Christmas Eve. In 2000 this happened, and I was scheduled to preach on that Sunday. I struggled with how to preach an Advent sermon (looking forward to the birth of Christ) when Christmas Eve was on the same day (celebrating the birth of Christ). I couldn't help thinking of Mary. What if she had begun her pregnancy with a visit to the home of Elizabeth (that morning), and just a few hours later she had given birth to the Christ Child (that evening). (I suspect more than one woman would like to have had her pregnancy shortened to just a few hours!)

As I pondered celebrating the fourth Sunday of Advent and Christmas Eve both on the same day, the thought of compression came to mind—compressing things together—such as the beginning of a pregnancy and the end of a pregnancy, both in one day. Mary's joyful exaltation and her pain at childbirth—together. Then I realized that was precisely the way I had been feeling at the time—pressed on every side. In addition to my priestly duties, which included writing a difficult sermon, I had been struggling for weeks to complete a thesis I was writing for my Doctor of Ministry degree in congregational development. That week, with a great burst of energy I finished my thesis, put it in the mail, and, to celebrate, my wife and I went to see the Tom Hanks movie *Cast Away.*

I found the film to be a profound commentary on contemporary life. In the story, Hanks plays the role of a high-speed manager for FedEx, who travels around the world to keep branch operations in line. He has a pager on his hip, a cell phone in one hand, and an electronic organizer in the other. Push-push-push is his way of life. The company has only to beckon, and he is on the next flight out. Work comes first, and relationships are a distant second.

On a flight back from Russia, a flight attendant asks another employee about the man's wife, who is terminally ill and dying of cancer. The attendant listens intently as the man shares his grief. She then puts her hand on his shoulder and tells him, "We are all thinking about you."

Everyone, that is, but Hanks. He has no time for relationships, not even with the woman he hopes to one day marry. As he races to leave on his next flight, she pleads for him to return soon, and he makes a promise that he will not be able to keep. His plane crashes in the Pacific Ocean, and Hanks finds himself alone on an island, a castaway. He tries to escape, but the ocean beats him back. Hanks gives up, realizing he will spend the rest of his life on a deserted island with nothing but coconuts to keep him company. Yet, the "cast away" experience becomes the container that molds and shapes Hanks for the better.

Mary, the mother of Jesus, had a container too—her pregnancy. It was the pressure cooker that would either cause her to shake her fist in the face of God or cause her to trust in God alone. Make no mistake;

either could have happened. Mary was as human as Zechariah, the priest, who also had been visited by an angel of the Lord, Gabriel. Gabriel had told Zechariah that his wife, Elizabeth, would bear a son, to be named John. The same angel told Mary that she would bear a son to be named Jesus.

Two people visited by the same angel, told the same thing, but with very different responses. Zechariah did not believe and was struck mute. Mary was different. She believed the angel and said, "Let it be with me according to your word." (See Luke 1:5-38). The story continues in Luke 1:39-56, where two expectant mothers—Elizabeth and Mary—visit to share the joys of being pregnant. Scripture tells us that the moment Elizabeth saw Mary and heard Mary's greeting, the baby in Elizabeth's womb "leaped for joy" (verse 44).

A strange story to be included in Scripture. Why all the details about Mary hurrying to the hill country, a baby leaping in his mother's womb? I believe the story is included in order to make a profound theological statement. Zechariah represents those who do not believe, who remain silent and are mute concerning Jesus. Elizabeth and Mary represent all who proclaim that he is the Messiah. That is why it was Elizabeth and not Zechariah who sang to Mary and child: "Blessed are you among women, and blessed is the fruit of your womb" (verse 42). Elizabeth's song prompted Mary to sing as well. Notice, Elizabeth praised Mary, but Mary gave praise to God when she sang her "Magnificat": "My soul magnifies the Lord, / and my spirit rejoices in God my Savior" (Luke 1:46-47). And why does Mary rejoice in God? Because the Lord "has looked with favor on the lowliness of his servant" (verse 48). Mary recognized what was taking place in her was the work of God.

Some of us know that the things taking place in our life indicate God is at work in us, too. And those things don't all have to be wonderful and exciting, either. Our present situation—even though it may be painful—may be God's opportunity, God's knocking at the door of our heart, God's seeking to transform our life. Others may say, "Perhaps that is true for others, but my situation is too difficult." Those who feel that way should consider Mary's plight. She didn't have much to sing about. She was a young, pregnant teenager. She was engaged but not yet married. When Joseph learned she was pregnant, he wanted to quietly divorce her. In first-century Judea—as has been true for almost every culture throughout human history—a woman being pregnant out of wedlock was reproached by others. She could easily have become a social outcast, a woman of the street.

Tom Hanks's movie *Cast Away* is the universal story of every person who has ever found himself or herself in an impossible situation in life. He is alone on a deserted island in the middle of the Pacific Ocean with absolutely no way of escape. Systematically, Hanks is stripped of everything that ever gave meaning in his former life—everything! And, when he is totally helpless and unable to do anything to change his situation, he has his epiphany. Then and only then is he able to escape his prison. He returns home a different man. *Cast Away* is a story of redemption, restoration, and transformation.

Near the end of the movie there is a poignant scene in which Hanks is sitting with the same fellow employee he was with at the beginning of the movie—the one whose wife was near the point of death. The man tells Tom that they all had thought he was dead—they even had a burial service for him. Hanks looks at the man and asks, "You had two burial services, didn't you? One for me and one for your wife." The man nodded in agreement and dropped his head. Hanks said, "I'm so sorry. I should have been there for you." It was a genuine moment from a man who had been unable to relate and genuinely care for other people. For me, the movie was itself a container that compressed into two-plus hours the four-year story of this man's redemption. At the beginning of the movie, Hanks was living a desolate, impoverished life and didn't even know it. He had to be "cast away" in order to become human.

As I planned my sermon I thought about a truly human experience we had all shared at church the previous Sunday. The church was packed with parents, family, and friends who had come to witness our annual Christmas pageant. I loved seeing our children dressed up as Mary, Joseph, and the shepherds. I loved hearing them sing. I loved seeing a hundred or more little kids coming in dressed as angels. And sitting where clergy get to sit, I got to see the faces of the parents. Mothers and fathers, grandmothers and grandfathers were beaming from ear to ear and waving like crazy to get the attention of their child or grandchild—to let them know they were watching their performance, to let them know they were the apples of their eye. I especially loved it when the star of Bethlehem began to make its way down a rope from the balcony to the front of the church. Our three little wise men started out following the star, but soon they were ahead of the star—it was following them. *So what* if our wise men happened to beat the star to Bethlehem? It mattered not. Our children are special to us, and we are glad to see and hear them tell one more time the greatest story ever told. Genuine stuff—children teaching their parents the story of baby Jesus, and about his mother, Mary, who sang her song.

Interestingly, the song Mary sang is in the past tense. She sings as if the things promised to her have already happened. Six times she uses the past tense. She exalts God because God has already blessed her and has already extended his mercy to those who fear him. God has already lifted up the lowly. God has already filled the hungry with good things. Mary says these things have already happened, even before Jesus is born, while the Messiah is still in her abdomen. Mary's faith had enlarged to the point of absolute belief and total trust in God. For Mary, God had already fulfilled his promise to bring justice, righteousness, and redemption to all people.

In other words, Mary was able to see the beginning and the end of God's story compressed together, all at once. She saw Christ's first coming as the Babe of Bethlehem and his second coming at the end of Ages—both Advents compressed together and made one.

Faith can do that. Through the eyes of faith Mary recognized that in Jesus Christ, the kingdom of God has already broken in and is already taking place. Mary's song brings together the expectancy of Advent and the birth of the Christ Child. Mary's song makes them one—not unlike that day in 2000, with Advent in the morning and the celebration of Jesus' birth in the evening. I believe this means when we find ourselves pressed and compressed in the pressure cooker of life and think we have no place to turn—feeling we are a castaway in a throwaway society—even then, it is time to give thanks to God, for the kingdom of God is already breaking into our lives, and what God has promised to do is already taking place. It matters not if we see it happening, because God is faithful and God's promises are sure.

God planted hope in the heart of Mary. If God has planted hope in your heart, then rejoice, and know it is time for you to begin to sing Mary's song, "My soul magnifies the Lord, / and my spirit rejoices in God my savior," for Advent and Christmas have been compressed together and made one.

Chapter 11

Chad Hammett and In-Between Time

After his suffering he presented himself alive to them by many convincing proofs, appearing to them during forty days and speaking about the kingdom of God. While staying with them, he ordered them not to leave Jerusalem, but to wait there for the promise of the Father. "This," he said, "is what you have heard from me; for John baptized with water, but you will be baptized with the Holy Spirit not many days from now." . . . Then they returned to Jerusalem from the mount called Olivet, which is near Jerusalem, a sabbath day's journey away. When they had entered the city, they went to the room upstairs where they were staying, Peter, and John, and James, and Andrew, Philip and Thomas, Bartholomew and Matthew, James son of Alphaeus, and Simon the Zealot, and Judas son of James. All these were constantly devoting themselves to prayer, together with certain women, including Mary the mother of Jesus, as well as his brothers.

(Acts 1:3-5, 12-14)

*I*n-between time—we have all been there. We all know what it is like to stand between promise and the dream we hope for. This happened to me when I began the process to be on the clergy staff of St. Martin's church in Houston. I took one look at the great church (the largest Episcopal church in the United States), and I knew this was where I would love to be, but fulfillment of that dream was a long time in coming. I had two visits with the rector. Next, I took a battery of tests. Ultimately I was invited to meet the head of the search committee. We ate lunch together, and weeks passed. Next, I was told I needed to meet the entire search committee—only instead of this being one visit, they wanted to meet in three small groups. Weeks turned into months. Then, I was asked to meet with the rector and the entire search committee, together at the same time. More questions and more waiting. Finally, when I least expected it, I was called to ask when I would be ready to start work. When? I wanted to say, "Three months ago would have been just fine." Instead, I said, "The first of May sounds fine to me!"

In-between time can be waiting for a job to materialize. It can also be waiting for a friend to forgive you. It can be living under the cloud of an impending divorce or waiting for a pathology report after a biopsy.

As a surgeon I was forced to live in many in-between times with my patients. This was especially true in the season of Easter 1978. On May 14 of that year, I was thrust into an in-between time when three-year-old Chad Hammett was brought to the Emergency Room of my hospital, Schumpert Medical Center in Shreveport. Half of his face literally had been blown apart when a shotgun accidentally discharged. I will spare you the details, but what I will say is that while I had seen many trauma cases as a plastic surgeon, the devastation of Chad's face was beyond anything I had ever experienced. And with that little boy's eyes riveted on me, watching every move I made, I grabbed his hand, forced myself to smile, and said, "Chad, everything is going to be all right. We are all here to help you. We can fix this, don't worry."

In the operating room we were able to rotate tissue to cover the defect on the outside and placed skin grafts to line the inside of his mouth. A series of operations followed over the years. Often the surgery achieved what we had hoped for, but scar tissue fought us every step of the way, requiring additional surgery. In-between times can be short; they can also seem like they will never end.

Jesus' disciples found themselves in an in-between time after our Christ ascended to heaven to be with God (see Acts 1:6-11). For them it was a time of great uncertainty. In fear for their very lives, they stayed behind locked doors; and not knowing what to expect, they could only wait for their destiny to unfold.

This was not the first time of uncertainty for the disciples, nor their first time to experience separation from Jesus. Knowing his departure would be difficult for his disciples, Jesus prayed a very special prayer for them. John 17 records the prayer Jesus prayed just before his death. It has much to say to anyone who is in an in-between time in life. Jesus began his prayer saying that everything he had done in life was to bring glory to his heavenly Father. He then prayed that in his death God would be glorified, as well. When you and I are in the in-between times of life—like Jesus—we can place ourselves in God's hands and ask that all the pain, agony, and fear we experience—that this too—will bring glory to God.

The second thing we learn from Jesus' prayer is that even in the in-between times of life we still belong to God. Things may not appear to be that way, but the truth is we are still *at one* with Christ and with God, our heavenly Father. Wherever we may be we are still beloved of God who will never leave us or forsake us, because he loves us. Jesus' entire prayer is based on the absolute certainty of his relationship with God the Father. The same can be true for us. We all experience uncertainty in life; but in God all things are certain and sure.

The third thing we can know is that the Risen Christ is making intercession for us at the right hand of God. Jesus prayed, "Holy Father, protect them by the power of your name—the name you gave to me—so that they may be one, just as we are one." Our Lord sees us as being *at one* with him and *at one* with the Father at all times. Not just when we feel like it. Not just when everything is going our way. No, our unity with Jesus Christ is as certain as the oneness that exists in the Godhead between God the Father and God the Son. For all these reasons, when we find ourselves in "in-between times" we can know that everything we experience can bring glory to God.

In 1999, on Palm Sunday, following the 9:15 A.M. chapel service, I noticed several people had remained in their pew, and after the chapel had emptied, I made my way over to them. It was then that a young man turned to face me, stuck out his hand and said, "Do you remember who I am?" I said, "I sure do, Chad Hammett, but I can't believe you look so good." An image of Chad in the emergency room with his face half blown off flashed through my mind. I had not seen him in more than ten years. Chad had grown into manhood and although he had a scar across his cheek, to me he was the most handsome man I had ever seen. I marveled that he spoke normally, knowing his jaw had been shattered. I was thrilled to see him and kept saying, "You look so good."

Chad then said something I shall never forget. He said, "Dr. Graham I have known you were in Houston for several months now but I waited to come see you until I had received a letter this past week saying I have been accepted to attend the University of Texas Medical School in Galveston, and I wanted you to know that you are the reason I want to be a doctor." We embraced, and then Chad said, "Every night before surgery you would come by my hospital room and pray with me." He added, "You will never know the impact you and your wife had on me and my mother." To which I said, "And you will never know the impact you and your mother had on us."

I tell you this story to say I could easily have lived my life and never seen Chad again. But, I did and that's how I learned that God had used an in-between time to bless a little boy, who in turn blessed me. What I find most remarkable about this story is that God has taken a devastating event in the life of a young child—one that could easily have scared him emotionally for life—and turned for good.

Henri Nouwen wrote a little book entitled *The Wounded Healer,* in which he says that in our own woundedness we can become a source of life for others.[1] Chad Hammett was wounded as a child and now he will train to be a healer—a wounded healer. I am sure Chad will touch many lives by God's grace. The same thing is true for all of us, as well. God takes the tragedies of our lives, heals our wounds, and sends us out to bring healing to others. Yet, I suspect that, this side of heaven, we will rarely know when God has used us to bless someone.

Surely, this was true of Thomas Cranmer, the man who was responsible for overseeing the compiling of the Book of Common Prayer in 1549. When Queen Mary came to reign on the throne of England, she reinstated Roman Catholicism and forced Cranmer to sign a confession rejecting the Prayer Book. Being the Archbishop of Canterbury was not easy in a nation that was Protestant under one ruler and Roman Catholic under the next. Two years after Cranmer signed his rejection of the Book of Common Prayer, he surprised everyone by repudiating his own confession. Enraged, Mary ordered he be burned at the stake.

One day, as I pondered the sad ending to Cranmer's life it suddenly occurred to me that at the time of his death he would have thought that was the end not only of his own life but also the Book of Common Prayer. I am sure he never imagined that one day the prayer book he compiled would be used every day by churches in the Anglican communion around the globe.

---

1. Henri J. M. Nouwen, *The Wounded Healer: Ministry in Contemporary Society.* Garden City, NY: Image Books, 1972, p. 82-83.

In-between times are like that. They are deceptive. The enemy of our soul wants us to think everything is over— that we have failed and that life will never be the same again—yet the truth is God has a marvelous way of taking our in-between times—along with all our pain and suffering—and turning them into a blessing. And, that's why we Christians are able to say in every situation we find ourselves, "To God be the glory."

Chapter 12

Saints: Ordinary People Living Extraordinary Lives

When Jesus saw the crowds, he went up the mountain; and after he sat down, his disciples came to him. Then he began to speak, and taught them, saying, "Blessed are the poor in spirit, for theirs is the kingdom of heaven. Blessed are those who mourn, for they will be comforted. Blessed are the meek, for they will inherit the earth. Blessed are those who hunger and thirst for righteousness, for they will be filled. Blessed are the merciful, for they will receive mercy. Blessed are the pure in heart, for they will see God. Blessed are the peacemakers, for they will be called children of God. Blessed are those who are persecuted for righteousness' sake, for theirs is the kingdom of heaven. Blessed are you when people revile you and persecute you and utter all kinds of evil against you falsely on my account. Rejoice and be glad, for your reward is great in heaven, for in the same way they persecuted the prophets who were before you." (Matthew 5:1-12)

Several years ago, I asked a number of people if they had ever met a "saint." Everyone said they had. High on the list were mothers and grandmothers. Also mentioned were parents, aunts and uncles, and teachers and friends who had manifested God's love in a special way.

Saints are recognized as having the qualities Jesus described in his Sermon on the Mount (Matthew 5–7). That's why the beatitudes—Jesus' series of blessings found in Matthew 5:3-12—are always read on All Saints' Day. The English word for "saint" comes from the Latin word *sanctus*, a word that means "holy." We repeat the *sanctus* during Holy Eucharist when we say, "Holy, Holy, Holy" in Holy Communion. Earthly things become "holy" and sacred when set apart for God's use.

In the Old Testament, the children of Israel took wood, metal, and cloth to construct a Tabernacle in the wilderness. In Christianity, we consecrate buildings and set them apart for holy use—the sacred space in which we worship. In Holy Communion in the Episcopal Church, a priest takes ordinary bread and wine and consecrates them, so that they are transformed into the body and blood of Christ, asking that we may "be made one body with him, that he may dwell in us and we in him." And as Christians, we commit our hearts and lives unto God in Christ, and every life that is committed to our Lord Jesus Christ is holy.

Yes, people can be holy. Many of them are honored in the stained-glass windows of churches. There we see depicted Jesus, his mother Mary, Elizabeth, the twelve disciples, and the apostle Paul, along with early church leaders such as Athanasius and Constantine, St. Alban, and St. Augustine. There have been great leaders in every tradition. We have Anglican heroes, too—people such as Thomas Cranmer (mentioned in the last chapter), who oversaw the formulation of our Book of Common Prayer; Samuel Seabury, the first bishop of the Episcopal Church; and Bishop Leonidas Polk, the missionary bishop who brought Christianity to Louisiana and to Texas.

When I think about saints, I always think of the Right Reverend William J. Cox, retired Suffragan Bishop of Maryland. Cox served as an assistant bishop in the Diocese of Texas, and it was my joy to serve with him for six months at St. Matthew's in Austin. Whenever the subject of saints came up, Bishop Cox would always say, "Saints are just ordinary people who lived extraordinary lives." I like that, because when we see people depicted in stained-glass windows, it is easy to think that saints are different from us, when they were all ordinary people just like you and me.

That's why I loved to hear the stories that Bishop Cox told. In one story, Father Philip P. B. Clayton, rector of a church in London, had gone to Africa on a preaching tour. When he returned to England, he was asked to speak on the BBC's radio network. In the interview, Father Clayton told the listening audience of seeing tens of thousands of persons with leprosy dying in Africa without medical attention.

Will Lambert, a wealthy industrialist, happened to be listening to this broadcast, and he was so touched by what he heard that one month later, he called Father Clayton to inform him he had sold his business and was enrolling in Guy's Hospital in London to train to become a medical missionary to Africa. Will Lambert fulfilled his commitment and spent twenty years as a medical missionary in Africa, treating over 1,000 persons with leprosy each year. He was responsible for saving over 20,000 men, women, boys, and girls from the ravages of this horrible disease. Bishop Cox ended his story by saying, "Will Lambert is one of the saints of God." He was an ordinary man who was used by God to do extraordinary things.

Saints do extraordinary things, but they are also recognized by their character. Humility and gentleness, generosity and faithfulness—these are some of the qualities that have caused people to identify certain men and women in every generation as saints. They are people who manifest the unconditional love of God to everyone. They are also true and steadfast in their faith—you can count on them. They include people such as St. Francis and Clare of Assisi, like St. Gregory of Nazianzus and Catherine of Sienna, and Ambrose of Milan, whose life and witness led to the conversion of St. Augustine of Hippo.

In the Anglican tradition, we have William Laud, who sought to place the Communion Table, rather than the pulpit, at the center of the church and encountered such violence at the hands of Puritans that he was imprisoned, accused of offensive practices, and beheaded on Tower Hill in London on January 10, 1645. Then too, there was William Tyndale, a humble parish priest who translated the Bible so his parishioners could read God's Word in their native language, English. When his bishop learned of this, Tyndale was tried as a heretic and burned at the stake. Yet, his translation of the Bible blessed countless Christians long after he was dead.

Another Anglican was John Keble, the shepherd of the Oxford Movement of the nineteenth century—a movement to revitalize the Church of England in his day. The Oxford Movement eventually touched the hearts of the founders of Alcoholics Anonymous in this country and led to the twelve-step movement that became such an important part of recovery for so many.

Ordinary men and women, doing extraordinary things by God's grace. All of this points to another characteristic of saints. They appear to seem instinctively to know their calling, and they have the ability to remain focused on the work that God has given. They aren't sidetracked by flattery or by the world's agenda. They know who they are and the gifts God has given. They take these gifts and use them to demonstrate that with God, all things are possible. And, the fact is, with God all things are possible even for ordinary folks like you and me. Like those who have gone on before, we are called to take what God has given, give it back to God, and allow God to so transform our lives that we can be used to touch others for Christ.

Our image may never be etched in the stained glass of a church window. Our name may never be recorded in the Oxford Dictionary of Saints. But of this I am certain: Our deeds will never be forgotten by God, and our deeds will never be forgotten by the *people* of God, either.

This leads me to another of Bishop Cox's stories. It is the story of Nellie Robinson, a story I could never forget. Nellie lived and died in the poverty-stricken Cumberland region of the United States. She died without ever knowing that one day her story would be told to me in far-away Austin, Texas. Never in her wildest dreams would Nellie ever have imagined that her story would be told on All Saints' Sunday to people in St. Martin's in Houston, the largest Episcopal church in the nation. Nor could she ever imagine her story would be written in this book for all to see. Indeed, she is not forgotten.

Nellie Robinson was seventy-five years old when Father Cox came as a young priest to the small Mission church in her hometown. Nellie lived in a little three-room "shotgun" house across the street from the church. Every Saturday she would bring her broom and mop to clean the church at no charge. As she scrubbed and mopped, Nellie filled the church with music as she sang songs of praise to God.

Although Nellie was a widow and never had children of her own, she raised eleven, and she lived to see all but four graduate from college. Not long after Father Cox arrived, he learned that her total income was from a monthly government pension check of only seventy-five dollars. The day came when the new priest invited his parish to pledge to give a portion of their income during the coming year. When the pledge cards came in, Nellie had signed one. She had pledged to give two dollars a week. Bishop Cox says he immediately realized that Nellie had pledged to give 11 percent of her meager income to the church. He was concerned as to whether or not she would have enough to live on and pay her medical bills. So, he went to her and said, "Nellie, you do so much for the church already. You clean it every week at no charge. Why don't you just let that be your gift?"

Nellie reacted instantly and said, "Oh, Father, please don't take this from me! Please don't stop me from giving to the Lord's work." Bishop Cox said from that time on, he has always taken more seriously the offerings anyone makes to God's work, no matter their situation in life.

Years later, Father Cox had become a bishop, and one day he learned that Nellie had died and had wanted him to officiate at her burial. At the cemetery, Bishop Cox learned that Nellie would be buried in a county plot for the indigent. Rain was falling in a heavy downpour, and there was no canopy over the gravesite, so the hole in the ground was half filled with water. Nellie was buried in a cheap pine box, and as her body was dropped into the water, the box floated for a few moments and finally sank beneath the surface. Bishop Cox says he remembers that service as the most joyful funeral he has ever experienced because that day, he knew with absolute certainty that Nellie Robinson had gone to be with her Lord and that Jesus was waiting with open arms to welcome this woman to her heavenly home.

Nellie was buried in a pauper's grave, but was she forgotten? Not at all. Like all the saints, Nellie was not forgotten by God, nor has her story been forgotten by the people of God. We tell her story just as we tell the stories of other saints—to bless us, to encourage us, and to build our faith.

You may never have thought about it, but one day the next generation of people in our churches will be telling our stories. The fact is, we are the saints of God in this generation, and every day we are living out the very stories the next generation will tell. Stories about the work you and others did to build or to help refurbish the place where you now worship. Stories about the Habitat for Humanity houses you helped to build so that persons in need would have a home. Stories about the hospitality you and others showed, which enabled important events and meetings to take place in your local area. And stories of how you gave of your time, talents, and possessions so that countless ministries could take place to bless the people of your church, your community, your nation, and far beyond.

"Ever met a saint?" Yes, you have. Saints are ordinary people who are doing extraordinary things by God's grace. And I want to be one, too.

Chapter 13

My Satellite TV, Resentment, and *The Green Mile*

John said to him, "Teacher, we saw someone casting out demons in your name, and we tried to stop him, because he was not following us." But Jesus said, "Do not stop him; for no one who does a deed of power in my name will be able soon afterward to speak evil of me. Whoever is not against us is for us. For truly I tell you, whoever gives you a cup of water to drink because you bear the name of Christ will by no means lose the reward." (Mark 9:38-41)

Several years ago I became distressed with the cable TV signal I was receiving at my home. Every time it rained, half of the channels became distorted. I really didn't care about most of those channels, but I cared a lot about channel 51. It carried the Houston Astros baseball games, and that channel was affected the worst of all. When it rained, I saw two images. I had to watch the Astros and a shopping channel at the same time. Jeff Bagwell was at bat, and a woman was trying to sell a string of pearls for three payments of $49.95.

At that precise moment, satellite TV became very attractive to me. The company promised a perfect picture and hundreds of channels to boot. A few days later, I had a satellite dish installed on my roof. As promised, every channel had crystal-clear reception. Only one problem: Rarely could I find my beloved Astros. Though I had purchased the local channels and a sports option, channel 51 was not included. I could watch the Atlanta Braves or the Los Angeles Giants, but not "my" team. And when an Astros game was scheduled, more often than not, the channel guide claimed the game was blacked out—even when the Astros were playing the Mets in faraway New York City, not in Houston.

Hearing me grumble, my wife finally said, "Why don't you call the company?" I wasn't about to tell her I had already called a dozen times and had gotten one of those recorded messages: "Push 1 on your touch pad if you are calling to purchase a system; push 2 if you need repairs." When I finally did get a human being on the line, it was someone who had no understanding of baseball, much less the Astros. "But sir, you can watch the Yankees and Cincinnati." I tried to tell her that I didn't care what happened to the Yankees, I was only interested in the Astros. She kept telling me the game was blacked out, and I kept saying, "Blacked out in New York, but not everywhere! They are playing in New York City. I should be able to see the game in Houston!"

All this leads me to admit that I had developed a slight degree of resentment toward my satellite TV company. I soon envisioned myself taking the entire system and dropping it on their desk in front of new customers—without my clerical collar, of course. Then, I discovered that the company never published their office address. I had placed my order over the telephone. The fact is, I didn't know where to return the system if I wanted to. My heart was stewing in resentment, and I wasn't ready for God to help me deal with it.

Resentment may well be what Jesus' disciples had to deal with in Mark 9. We are told that John reported to Jesus, "Teacher, we saw someone casting out demons in your name, and we tried to stop him, because he was not following us."

Interestingly, this is the only place in all four Gospels where John is mentioned alone. Everywhere else, he is mentioned along with other disciples—usually Peter and James. But in this passage, John's name is mentioned alone, which provides the opportunity to observe this disciple's attitude and behavior up close.

First of all, we need to know that earlier in the same chapter of Mark's Gospel, the disciples had attempted to heal a boy with epilepsy and failed. Get the picture? John was unable to heal, but an outsider—a man who wasn't even one of Jesus' disciples—was praying in Jesus' name and casting out demons easily. And another thing, the disciples had been trying to decide who was the greatest among them. How could they say any of Jesus' disciples was the greatest when an outsider was able to heal people, and they couldn't? This was insult upon injury.

How did John react to this man who was healing people in Jesus' name? Scripture records that John reported he "tried" to stop him, which means John didn't succeed. Can't you see John trying to stop the man? Telling him, "Stop it! I said, Stop it! You are not one of us. You have no right to use Jesus' name to cast out demons!" Can't you just feel the embarrassment John must have felt? This stranger completely ignored John and went right on healing people.

Humiliated in public, John then ran to Jesus, surely expecting that the Lord would be upset to learn someone was using his name without his approval. After all, this guy was practicing medicine without a license. He had no plaque on the wall. He was a renegade and a charlatan, no less. "Jesus, you had better stop this man before things get completely out of control. Soon, *everyone* will be healing in your name! We can't have *that,* can we?"

Jesus must have shocked John to the core of his being when he said, "Don't stop the man, for no one who performs a miracle in my name will be able to speak evil of me."

What had happened to John? I believe his understanding had become distorted due to his own bitterness and resentment. What was Jesus doing? Like always, Jesus had to turn the world of his disciples upside-down in order to shatter their narrow perceptions, just as Jesus wants us to expand our vision to include other people and to know that our way of doing things may not always be God's way.

Back to my own resentment. While studying for a class I was teaching, I happened to read Hebrews 12:15, which says, "Pursue peace with everyone." And I knew that had to include my satellite TV company. The next verse says, "See to it that no one fails to obtain the grace of God; that no root of bitterness springs up and causes trouble, and through it many become defiled." "Root of bitterness"? I had an entire *tree* of bitterness—a spreading oak tree, at that. Reluctantly, I asked God to forgive me and to give me a new heart, and God did.

The burden of my sin lifted, and not long after praying that prayer an interesting thing happened. As long as I had been focused on the Astros and on their absence from my satellite-TV programming, my vision had been blocked and I was unable to appreciate all that the new system had to offer. For one thing, I could now order pay-per-view movies without having to go out to the video-rental store. Just press a button, and the movie of my choice was right there on the screen.

Like the movie *The Green Mile,* the story of a gentle giant of a man named John Coffey, spelled C-o-f-f-e-y. "Like the drink, only not spelled the same," he always said. Coffey was on death row for the murder of two little girls. When arrested, he was holding the bodies of the two girls in his arms. Only, he was not the killer; John Coffey had been trying to bring them back to life.

As the movie unfolds, we learn that Coffey has an extraordinary gift of healing, and can exorcise pain and affliction from people by extracting it out of the other person, taking it into his own lungs and exhaling it out again. After Coffey heals the warden's wife, who is dying of a brain tumor, it is revealed to Tom Hanks—the veteran death row prison guard—that they are about to execute an innocent man. Hanks goes to the prosecuting attorney only to learn that the man will not reopen the case. The prosecutor shows Hanks his ten-year-old son, whose face was severely disfigured when he was attacked by the family dog. The man says that you can never tell when a gentle dog will become violent. "John Coffey may be gentle today, but don't turn your back on him or you will live to regret it."

Unable to stop the execution, in a powerful scene Hanks tells Coffey, "On the day of my judgment, when I stand before God, and He asks me why did I kill one of his true miracles, what am I gonna say?" *The Green Mile* tells the story of how resentment can distort one's perception and prevent us from seeing the truth.

Resentment caused me to want to throw my satellite dish on the trash heap. Resentment caused one of Jesus' disciples to try to stop a man—a man like John Coffey in the movie—a man who only wanted to heal people. The fact is, a root of bitterness and resentment can fester in the heart of anyone who has been hurt, wounded, or humiliated. None of us is immune, including Jesus' most beloved disciple.

Let that happen, and resentment can prevent a person from recognizing and celebrating the things that God is doing, strange things and in strange places—like an outsider casting out demons in Jesus' name. Like members of one church teaching a second language to immigrants at another church. Like a local hospital giving away millions of dollars every year through charities to improve the medical care of the poor and homeless. Like people in churches and synagogues all over America giving of their time and talent and money to help others throughout our nation.

Yes, "strange" things in strange places. Could it be that these people have heard God calling in the night and have obeyed? "Stop them," you say? Oh no, don't stop them. Instead, go and do likewise.

Chapter 14

"Go-Forwards"

[Jesus said,] "I am the bread of life. Your ancestors ate the manna in the wilderness, and they died. This is the bread that comes down from heaven, so that one may eat of it and not die. I am the living bread that came down from heaven. Whoever eats of this bread will live forever; and the bread that I will give for the life of the world is my flesh. . . . Those who eat my flesh and drink my blood have eternal life, and I will raise them up on the last day."

(John 6:48-51, 54)

I love to spend time with family and friends. Recently, our daughter, Ginger, and our son-in-law, David Knight, came for a visit with their four boys. One afternoon I was playing with their two-year-old son, Graham, when he pointed up to the corner of the room and asked, "Why that song broke?" Puzzled, I asked him to repeat what he had said. Pointing toward the corner, he said, "Why that song broke?" Then I realized he was pointing at one of the speakers I had hung in the corner of the room to create a surround-sound effect. "Do you want to listen to music?" I asked, and he said, "Uh-huh!"

I was fascinated by this. My two-year-old grandson had renamed a speaker a "song." He probably gets it from me. I rename things all the time. Once, I asked my wife if she knew where I had put my "go-forwards." "Go-forwards"? she asked. "Yes, you know—those rubber-slipper-like-things you wear at the beach." "Do you mean, *thongs*" (also known as "flip-flops")? "Yes, thongs, and they are 'go-forwards,' too, because if you try to go backwards, they will slip off your feet. You can only go *forward* in 'go-forwards.'" That day, thongs became "go-forwards" in our house.

The power to name a thing is very Hebrew. The Bible begins with God at Creation, speaking and naming the sun, the moon, and the stars. Adam is instructed to name the animals in the garden. In the Old

Testament, the Lord God renames Abram, *Abraham,* and when Jacob wrestles with the angel, his name is changed to *Israel.* In the New Testament, Jesus renames Simon *Peter;* and on the road to Damascus, Saul is renamed *Paul.*

Transfiguration Sunday celebrates the day Jesus was gloriously transfigured before his disciples on a mountaintop. (See Matthew 17:1-13; Mark 9:2-8; and Luke 9:28-36.) Moses and Elijah were there too, and Scripture says they talked with Jesus about his coming departure—that he would soon be rejected, would suffer, and would die. Coming down from that mountain, Jesus set his face like flint straight for Jerusalem, where an amazing thing happened. Although Jesus knew he was about to die, he did not react against those who were about to crucify him. Instead, Jesus transformed death itself. Jesus did not allow others to define him. Instead, he took a piece of bread, held it up, and with all the authority in heaven and on earth, he renamed that piece of bread, saying, "This is my body"; and, lifting a cup of wine, he said, "This is my blood."

It is amazing; knowing full well that soon, people would try to kill him, Jesus did not soften his message or make it more palatable. Instead, he made it even more difficult for anyone to follow him when he said, "You must eat my flesh and drink my blood." God has a way of doing that—rather than appeasing us, God raises the bar one notch higher, and in the process forces us to decide whether we will allow him to be the solid rock upon which we stand or the stone upon which we stumble. Jesus forced people to accept him on his terms, not theirs.

"You must eat my flesh and drink my blood," he said. Eat his flesh? Drink his blood? Didn't Jesus know Jewish law forbade anyone from drinking blood? Didn't he know that every civilized nation on earth has forbidden the eating of human flesh? Was he insane?

"Eat my flesh and drink my blood" is Eucharist talk, isn't it? The words we say at the distribution of the elements come readily to mind: "This is the body of Christ, the bread of heaven; this is the blood of Christ, the cup of salvation." Anglicans don't pretend to be able to explain what happens at Holy Communion. What happens is in God's hands. What we do affirm is that in the sacrament of Holy Communion, Christ is present. When we eat the bread and drink the wine, we are united with Jesus Christ in the most essential and elemental way possible; and somehow in that simple act of obedience—doing what

Jesus has asked us to do—we become one with Christ, "we in him and he in us."

What is Jesus asking of us when he says we are to eat his flesh and drink his blood? I believe God is asking us to assimilate Christ into our very being—to receive Christ and his Spirit into our heart, mind, and soul, into every aspect of our being. Receive Christ, so we will be transformed and become like Christ. So we will love what Christ loves. As the early church founders said, those who receive the body and blood of Christ become a "little Christ"—little Christs who are called, as the Jewish nation was called, to be God's instruments in the world.

Jesus said if we do that—if we eat his flesh and drink his blood—we will live forever. That is our Lord's promise, and for two thousand years now, we have come to the Lord's Table; people of all ages—men and women, little children with their parents; people who are rich and people who are poor; people who are brilliant and people who are intellectually challenged; young adults vibrant with life itself and older adults barely able to walk down the church aisle. We come Sunday after Sunday because we believe that what Jesus has said is true—that if we partake of his body and blood, we will be united with him and will dwell with him forever.

I have thought a lot about what my grandson did—rename my stereo speaker a "song." And the more I think about it, I believe Graham has it right. The purpose of that speaker is to make music, so calling it a song is appropriate. Making music is the function of that speaker. You and I have a function too. We are to be so united to Jesus Christ that we will make the music God wants each of us to make.

That being true, it seems to me we should be renamed. I would rename the people of God as "Go-forwards." Yes, "go-forwards," because we have slipped our feet into Jesus' sandals and have decided to go forward with him. Just as Jesus set his face like a flint toward Jerusalem and the cross, never turning back, so we have set our face toward the things of God and will never turn back.

One thing is certain, we'll never go backwards if we walk with Jesus. Jesus is a go-forward person! "Go-forwards," people who are united with Jesus Christ, have eaten his body and have drunk of his blood, and will never look back. For me, that's who we are—"Go-forwards."

At St. Martin's, from time to time our prayer ministry team provides the opportunity to walk the labyrinth, an ancient form of walking meditation and contemplative prayer. When you walk the labyrinth, you begin with the palms of your hands turned upward toward heaven, and with each step you empty yourself before God. The path wanders back and forth until you reach the center, where you sit on cushions and open your heart to God, listening for God's voice. On your way out, you hold your hands face down, implying you will now give to others what you have received. For many, walking the labyrinth is a powerful experience.

One day it occurred to me that when you walk the labyrinth, you are always going forward. The labyrinth is not a maze. There are no blind alleys, so you never go backwards—you always go forward. Staying on the path does require that you turn and go in the opposite direction repeatedly—as we do when we repent of sin—but you always walk forward. For me, the labyrinth is a beautiful metaphor for a go-forward people, a people who have set their face like flint to follow God. Yet for many, life seems to be more a maze than a labyrinth, with blind alleys at every turn. Despair can easily overwhelm a person who comes to believe there is no hope for change.

Perhaps the most touching funeral service I have ever witnessed was that of a young man who had suffered from mental illness and, believing he would never get well again, tragically took his own life. We knew the family. They were wonderful people who had done everything they could to support their son. I will never forget how at the end of the service, a long stream of young adults came down the aisle, and one by one touched the young man's casket. Tears filled every eye in the room as we pondered this tragic loss of life.

Near the end of the service the choir began to sing a contemporary Christian worship hymn written by D. J. Butler in 1987, called "I Will Change Your Name" (© Mercy Publishing Co.). In this song, God gently speaks to you, the listener, letting you know that no longer will you be identified by the brokenness, the fear, and the pain that you have carried with you in the past. Instead, God has given you a new name, a name that reflects the joy of a life to be lived in God, a name that identifies you as a "friend of God, one who sees my face."

It was a powerful experience for us all as we recalled the book of Revelation, which says that death will not have the final say over God's people—*God* will. Just as Jesus did not allow those who crucified him to establish the meaning of his death, neither will God allow the pain of this world to define us. No, Revelation says that God will write a new name on the foreheads of his people, a name that only God knows. No longer will we be called by the name of our old life. We belong to God, and our new name will be "joyfulness," "friend of God." With that as our hope, we can be "go-forwards"—people who "go forward" with God, wherever God may lead.

Chapter 15

Yoko Ono's Wish Tree and Prayer

[Jesus] was praying in a certain place, and after he had finished, one of his disciples said to him, "Lord, teach us to pray, as John taught his disciples." He said to them, "When you pray, say: Father, hallowed be your name. / Your kingdom come. / Give us each day our daily bread. / And forgive us our sins, / for we ourselves forgive everyone indebted to us. / And do not bring us to the time of trial." And he said to them, "Suppose one of you has a friend, and you go to him at midnight and say to him, 'Friend, lend me three loaves of bread; for a friend of mine has arrived, and I have nothing to set before him.' And he answers from within, 'Do not bother me; the door has already been locked, and my children are with me in bed; I cannot get up and give you anything.' I tell you, even though he will not get up and give him anything because he is his friend, at least because of his persistence he will get up and give him whatever he needs. So I say to you, Ask, and it will be given you; search, and you will find; knock, and the door will be opened for you. For everyone who asks receives, and everyone who searches finds, and for everyone who knocks, the door will be opened. Is there anyone among you who, if your child asks for a fish, will give a snake instead of a fish? Or if the child asks for an egg, will give a scorpion? If you then, who are evil, know how to give good gifts to your children, how much more will the heavenly Father give the Holy Spirit to those who ask him!"

(Luke 11:1-13)

When the musical group The Beatles came onto the scene in the 1960s, I must confess, I was offended by them. I didn't like their lyrics, their clothes, or their lifestyle. I was upset by what I thought was their arrogance when John Lennon said their group had more influence than Jesus Christ. I was turned off when they went to India to sit at the feet of a Yogi Master, instead of going to a church. When John Lennon married Yoko Ono, in my mind they were birds of a feather and she had absolutely nothing to say to me.

In the summer of 2001, Houston's Contemporary Art Museum gave a showing of Yoko Ono's work. I decided to go see the exhibit because at the time I was on vacation, and when on vacation, I always want to do something totally different, something I don't ordinarily do. Ono's exhibit was the opposite of anything I had ever done in my life, so it seemed to fit the bill.

Much of her work affirmed my prejudice. There was a motion picture of the backside of a naked man walking down the street. There was a video of a fly walking around on the body of a woman. The sound a fly makes was magnified a thousand times. I thought, "Just what I needed to experience on my vacation—a naked man walking down the street and a fly sniffing someone's body while I am forced to listen to the fly's amplified screeching."

Nevertheless, walking around the exhibit I learned things about Yoko Ono and John Lennon that humanized them for me. Ono was born in Japan and was in Tokyo when the city was bombed during World War II, and when the atomic bombs were dropped on Nagasaki and Hiroshima. This helped me appreciate her efforts for world peace, which previously I had thought were part of a plot to disarm our nation. With a better understanding of Ono, I began to appreciate what she was trying to do with her art.

In the mid-1950s, Ono moved from Japan to New York City to be a part of the contemporary art movement there and to learn from the American artist John Cage. Cage rejected the techniques of classical oil painting to say that art is around us every day of our lives but goes unnoticed. A tub in the bathroom, the sink in the kitchen, the broom in the broom-closet—these are works of art if we have eyes to see and ears to hear.

Ono accepted Cage's ideas and also wanted to emphasize the participation of the audience. For that reason, many of her works were designed to be completed by those who came to view her art. For example, once she painted a wooden board white, attached a small hammer with a chain, and offered the viewer a bowl of nails. People were to use the hammer to drive a nail into the board. At the end of the exhibit, the "painting" was considered finished, and the audience had participated in its creation. And you know what? The longer I looked at that board, the more I wanted to take that hammer and drive in a nail myself. I wanted to be a participant too. I wanted to help create that painting.

In 1990, Ono went even further. She installed a large wooden cross in Judson Memorial Church in New York City. Viewers were invited to climb a ladder and drive a nail into the cross. I don't know the impact this had on the people at that church, but what immediately came to my mind was the verse in Paul's letter to the Colossians that says while we were dead in our sins, "God made [us] alive together with [Christ], when he forgave us all our trespasses. . . . He set this aside, nailing it to the cross" (Colossians 2:13-14, adapted). I also recalled the words to a hymn entitled "It Is Well with My Soul." I have sung it a thousand times in my life, and particularly the third verse came to mind: "My sin, oh, the bliss of this glorious thought! My sin, not in part but the whole, is nailed to the cross, and I bear it no more, praise the Lord, praise the Lord, O my soul!" Yoko Ono said that driving a nail in the cross had an atoning effect upon her, as she thought of the many martyrs who had died throughout human history

The exhibit also included a chair wrapped in cloth. What a strange thing to call art, I thought, until I learned Ono uses the wrapping of objects because it is a very feminine thing to do—women wrap babes in swaddling cloths (I thought of Jesus), nurses wrap wounds (I thought of my days in the operating room), and mothers wrap their arms around a child who is crying (I thought of my mother, who held me many times). Ono presented her audience with a chair painted white and a basket filled with rolls of gauze. She asked the people to do whatever they wanted to do to complete the work. Hesitantly at first, one by one they began to wrap the chair in the gauze. As I looked at their creation, I could almost feel emotion bound in the layers of gauze. The chair was no longer just a chair. It became, for me, the chair that my mother used to sit in at her kitchen table as she cooked and waited for her family to come home. I was deeply touched.

As you exit the museum, you pass a final work called *Wish Tree*. You are invited to write down your wish on a card and attach it to the Wish Tree. Being curious, I began reading the cards that hung on the tree. Several wished for money. One said, "I wish for $1,000,000 dollars by tomorrow." Another said, "I wish I was a princess." Another, "I wish my website would become a huge success." Still another said, "I wish I knew what to wish for." Most were more serious, dealing with personal relationships, family problems, and finding meaning in life. One card displayed a wish "to make a connection with someone, anyone." I realized this person was feeling desperately alone. Another read " . . . to find my calling in life." I had struggled with God's call upon my life for years, and I knew something of what that meant for this person. Yet another card said, " . . . to become pregnant." I have had friends who struggled to have a baby. I knew the pain and suffering they had endured. Then too, there was a note scribbled by a child: "I wish my mom would stop smoking!" Many wished for a cure for cancer, and some named the cancer specifically. I knew they had a loved one with that disease. Finally there were several generic wishes expressed for the end of world hunger and war.

As I drove home from the exhibit, I thought about Ono's Wish Tree and realized that each card said very little—just a few words—yet so much was expressed. We had been walking around the exhibit hall without saying anything to one another, and, because Ono had allowed us to participate in this way, people had expressed their heart and soul on a card for all the world to see—for the heavens to see. I understood then that each card was a prayer. Some were frivolous, but many were profound messages from the heart.

The notes on the wish tree may be prayers, but they are not to be mistaken for the prayer Jesus taught his disciples in the eleventh chapter of Luke. The Lord's Prayer is different. First of all, Jesus taught that we may bring our requests directly to God with the same confidence with which we would bring a request to a parent who loves us unconditionally, a parent who would wrap her arms about us and hold us close.

Jesus said, if your child asked for a fish, would you give him a snake instead? Of course you wouldn't. And if your child asked for an egg, would you give her a scorpion? Of course not. Then Jesus said, "If you then . . . know how to give good gifts to your children, how much more will the heavenly Father give the Holy Spirit to those who ask him!" (verse 13).

Jesus' Prayer begins with this kind of confidence when he says, "Our Father who art in heaven" (KJV). The word Jesus chose for "Father" is a word of intimacy used for one's earthly father. Jesus is saying that we can address the Lord God Almighty, Creator of heaven and earth, as "Father" because, indeed, we are God's children and we belong to him. Colossians says, not only have our sins been nailed to the tree, but we have also been united with Jesus Christ in his death, burial, and resurrection; and at Holy Baptism, we were marked as Christ's own forever. Knowing we are God's children means that we need have no fear or be timid when we come to God with our requests. The fact is, God loves for us to come to him in prayer.

What is effective prayer? Effective prayer is coming to God in faith, believing that God is a good God and that God will reward those who diligently seek him (see Hebrews 11:6). Effective prayer embraces God's kingdom and God's will for our life. Effective prayer boldly brings one's needs to God (see Hebrews 4:16) and asks God to be our healer, asks God to be the provider of our every need, asks God to protect us from the enemy of our soul. Effective prayer trusts that God will answer our prayers in the best way possible. And effective prayer rejoices ahead of time, knowing angels have already been dispatched and the answer to our prayer is already on the way.

Jesus said that if we pray as he taught us to pray, we can ask, and we will receive; we can search, and we will find; we can knock, and the door will be opened for us (see Luke 11:9). The three verbs Jesus uses here—*ask, search,* and *knock*—are all three in the present tense in the Greek text, indicating there is to be a continual asking, a continual searching, and a continual knocking on our part. It appears God is very interested in developing an ongoing, daily relationship with us—one that will transform us into the image of his dear Son. Prayer has that effect—we are changed when we pray, and that, I believe, is why God wants us to pray.

The centerpiece for Yoko Ono's exhibit is a ladder painted white, positioned beneath a white board that is suspended from the ceiling. A magnifying glass is hanging down by a chain from overhead. When first exhibited in 1966, individuals were asked to climb up the ladder and look through the magnifying glass. When they did, what they found was a word printed on the white board above them. To see that word you had to climb the ladder. To see the word you had to look upward. To see the word you had to diligently look and search through the magnifying glass. Those who looked upward found a single word above them. The word was *Yes.*

Ono's ladder reminded me of the ladder Jacob saw in his vision when he wrestled with the angel of God, and the word *Yes* is God's message to humanity. *Yes:* Ask, and you will receive; search, and you will find; knock, and the door will be opened for you. Better still—*keep on* asking, and you will receive. Keep on searching, and you will find. Keep on knocking, and the door will be opened for you! Twentieth-century theologian Karl Barth said that the resurrection of Jesus Christ is a great big, divine "Yes" from God to humanity. Others may reject us, but God will never reject us. God's word to you is—and always will be—YES!

I have thought a lot about Yoko Ono's exhibit. The theme of her work is participation—the artist and the viewer working together. Her art is not finished until the audience makes its contribution. To me, prayer is like that. Prayer is participation with the living God.

Someone put it this way: "Without God, we cannot; and without us, God will not." I wouldn't want to box God in and say what God will and will not do, but it does appear in this passage in Luke 11 that God will not act until God's people act—until we participate by praying that God's kingdom come on earth, in our own lives and in the lives of those we love. Seen this way, prayer is a glorious invitation to participate in bringing God's work to completion on planet Earth. What an awesome responsibility is prayer. What an awesome privilege as well.

And so we make our requests known to a God whose arm is not short and to a God who is ever willing to save. No wonder that, according to some ancient authorities, Jesus ended his prayer with a doxology, saying, "Thine be the kingdom and power and glory, for ever and ever. Amen."

Chapter 16

The Perfect Storm

On that day, when evening had come, he said to them, "Let us go across to the other side." And leaving the crowd behind, they took him with them in the boat, just as he was. Other boats were with him. A great windstorm arose, and the waves beat into the boat, so that the boat was already being swamped. But he was in the stern, asleep on the cushion; and they woke him up and said to him, "Teacher, do you not care that we are perishing?" He woke up and rebuked the wind, and said to the sea, "Peace! Be still!" Then the wind ceased, and there was a dead calm. He said to them, "Why are you afraid? Have you still no faith?" And they were filled with great awe and said to one another, "Who then is this, that even the wind and the sea obey him?" (Mark 4:35-41)

I suspect we can all identify with the fear the disciples must have experienced when a storm suddenly endangered their lives. I know I can.

Years ago when my wife and I lived in Shreveport, our home was just outside of town on a beautiful open-water lake. One weekend we had spent two beautiful days with our family, skiing on the lake and having fun. Around 4:00 on Sunday afternoon, I lit our outdoor cooker and was about to begin cooking when a violent thunderstorm struck without warning. I raced into the house and stood watching as rain began to come down in sheets, blown almost sideways by the force of the wind that was creating waves higher than the railing on the pier to our boathouse. I was concerned that our boathouse and ski boat would be destroyed.

These concerns vanished when I received a telephone call from my next-door neighbor, telling me that his son and our ten-year-old son, Patrick, had gone in a small boat to rescue a man who was on a sail-board in the middle of the lake. When last seen, they were headed in the direction of a marina several miles down the lake. Only, now the waves were higher than anyone had ever seen on Cross Lake, and no one could see their boat.

I called the marina and learned they were not there. Next, I called the shore patrol and asked them to send out a search party. I was told the storm was so severe they would have to wait until it was over to begin the search. In desperation, I got into my car and began racing up and down every side road between our home and the marina, looking for our neighbor's boat and the boys. Terror had filled my heart, and I cried out to God for help.

This is precisely the kind of situation in which the disciples found themselves. The waves coming at them were higher than the sides of their boat, and the vessel was about to sink. Where was Jesus? He was in the boat asleep. Talk about peace in the midst of a storm! When Jesus saw their situation, did he become afraid like his disciples? No. He spoke to the winds and the sea, and they became perfectly calm. He commanded the elements, and they obeyed him. Upon seeing this, Jesus' disciples were no longer afraid of the storm; now they were afraid of Jesus! They were afraid of the One who had this kind of power.

What does this passage have to say to us? The first thing I believe this story says to us is that to be human is suddenly to find ourselves in situations for which we are totally unprepared. This can happen any- where, anytime. A sudden storm can strike or the stock market can crash. We can find ourselves in the storm of a relationship or marriage that has gone sour. Our workplace can change overnight and we are forced to seek new employment. Parents can learn that their son or daughter is using drugs. A child can learn that his or her parents are seeking a divorce. We can discover a lump in our breast or an enlarged lymph node in our neck, experience chest pain, and have a massive heart attack or stroke. Our spouse or loved one can drop dead, flooding us in a sea of emotions.

The maddening thing about all of this is that moments before, we thought everything was perfectly fine, "clear sailing and sunny skies ahead." Or so we thought—and then suddenly everything has changed, and for the moment, it is impossible to believe anything can make things right again. Yes, the winds of life can rage with hurricane force, and we can find ourselves utterly helpless to do anything about it.

There is good news in Mark's Gospel—Jesus was in the boat with the disciples all along. When faced with catastrophe, all too often we think we are alone. We may even be justified in feeling this way, because our fair-weather friends have a way of deserting us when the going gets tough. Yet, even if everyone else disappears, we can know with assurance that Jesus is still in our boat with us. Following Jesus Christ doesn't mean we will have a storm-free existence. It didn't mean this for Jesus or his disciples, and it doesn't mean this for us, either. The fact is, Christ does not save us *from* storms, but God does join us *in* the storms of life. Ralph Waldo Emerson once said, "The wise man in the storm prays to God, not for safety from danger, but for deliverance from fear. It is the storm within which endangers him, not the storm without."

Yes, God saves us in the storms of life, and, just as important, this Gospel story in Mark 4 tells us how we are to live through these storms and get to the other side. First, we should acknowledge that there are storms in life that can be changed by sheer will. In these situations we are indeed the "captain" of our own "ship." Four years ago, two men were washing windows on the outside of a building in downtown Houston when a storm struck suddenly with hurricane-force winds. The two men held onto their platform for dear life until one of the men had the presence of mind to kick in a window, which allowed them to crawl to safety. Like that man, sometimes we can kick in a window and make our escape. We can apply for a new job if we have none. We can leave an abusive relationship.

Some storms can be solved by our own actions—doing what we know we need to do. But often when we try to change things, nothing works. There are times when the more we try to change things—or change people—the worse things get. We set out to manage these kinds of problems, and they wind up managing us. Yes, there are "storms" in life that simply will not respond no matter how much we may struggle. In these situations, the more we struggle, the more the wind beats against us. Soon, our sails are ripped apart and our mast is broken in two. We find ourselves in the grip of a darkness, and death seems to be knocking at the door.

The Perfect Storm is a movie that tells the story of a crew on a fishing boat, the *Andrea Gail,* far from shore, with a huge catch of fish. Just as they head back to shore, a hurricane named Grace is heading up the

Atlantic coastline. But Hurricane Grace is not the only storm they face. Another storm of epic proportions arises with such suddenness that the National Weather Bureau doesn't even have time to name it. This unnamed storm is more terrifying than one can imagine, greater than any storm on record—one that can send their tiny ship to the bottom of the sea. Death is knocking at the door, and The Perfect Storm is about to devour them all.

Life is like that, too, and in these situations we are wise to do exactly what the disciples did—call out to Jesus. The disciples were angry and shouted at Jesus, "Teacher, do you not care that we are perishing?" Not exactly a sweet little prayer, is it? No, but this kind of prayer faithfully expresses the pain and desperation we feel, and I have found that God is never offended by our heart's cry, a cry of desperation—a life-and-death scream for help. These prayers acknowledge that God can change any situation—nothing is too difficult for God. And when we realize that *we can't,* it is much easier to see that *God can.* When we find ourselves in situations where the more we do, the worse things get, the message of Mark 4 is to stand still, and ask Jesus to come in his power and do what we cannot do. In other words, simply "let go, and let God."

After I searched along the shoreline for at least thirty minutes and found no sign of my son and his friend or their boat, I went back home hoping the boys had already returned. They had not. A cloud of cold fear settled over me. In my mind's eye, there was no way they could have survived. I was certain they had drowned. Pat and I hugged, and cried a desperation cry for God to save our son. I had done everything I knew to do. Now, all I could do was "let go, and let God." It was an agonizing time. Minutes seemed like hours. When I had given up all hope, suddenly the telephone rang. A woman was calling to say that she had two very wet boys at her house. Half-way to the marina, the boys had pulled ashore with the man they had rescued. Our son did not die that day, but I have never forgotten the terror that storm brought to our household.

George Muller was a great prayer warrior of the nineteenth century, who said, "The beginning of anxiety is the end of faith, and the beginning of true faith is the end of anxiety." And Jeremy Taylor, whose two books *Holy Living* and *Holy Dying* are said to be the clearest expression of seventeenth-century Anglican spirituality, said this: "It is impossible for that man to despair who remembers that his Helper is omnipotent."

Knowing this to be true, I try to recall these four things when I find myself in the storms of life: First, I try to remember that it is truly the storm in my heart that endangers me more than any external storm I may encounter. Second, I remember that the one to whom I have given my heart—Jesus Christ—is the Son of the omnipotent God, who is able to deliver me at any moment. Third, I recall that the anxiety I have is due to lack of trust that God is present in my life. Fourth and finally, after I have done all I can do, it is time for me to let go and let God.

I believe that if we do these four things, we will see that Jesus has been "in our boat" all along. And knowing that Jesus is with us can give us the faith to hear him say, "Peace! Be still!" Just three little words, yet words so powerful that even the elements must obey. "Peace! Be still!" To hear these words is the end of all anxiety—three little words from Jesus that can calm our hearts and calm our lives as well.

Come to think of it, the moviemaker was wrong. The Perfect Storm is not on the high sea, way out there somewhere. No, The Perfect Storm is Jesus standing in the midst of the storm of my heart and in the storms of my life—Jesus, standing and saying, "Peace! Be still!"

Chapter 17

There Is Snoring in the House

"For as the days of Noah were, so will be the coming of the Son of Man. For as in those days before the flood they were eating and drinking, marrying and giving in marriage, until the day Noah entered the ark, and they knew nothing until the flood came and swept them all away, so too will be the coming of the Son of Man. Then two will be in the field; one will be taken and one will be left. Two women will be grinding meal together; one will be taken and one will be left. Keep awake therefore, for you do not know on what day your Lord is coming. But understand this: if the owner of the house had known in what part of the night the thief was coming, he would have stayed awake and would not have let his house be broken into. Therefore you also must be ready, for the Son of Man is coming at an unexpected hour."

(Matthew 24:37-44)

*I*n 1995, my wife, Pat, and I spent the Thanksgiving holidays with our daughter Cathey at her home in Shreveport. We had a wonderful visit, and knowing I would be preaching on the first Sunday of Advent, I read the Scripture lessons to my daughter. Cathey is a gifted writer, and I wanted to see what ideas she might have that could help my sermon preparation.

The only help I got was when I came to the epistle reading from Romans 13:8-14, which read, in part, "The night is far gone, the day is near" (verse 12). When I read that phrase, Cathey broke out laughing and said, "The night is far gone, and there is snoring in our house."

"Snoring in our house"? What you have to know is that there has been a long-standing conspiracy in my family to falsely accuse me of being a snorer. I knew better. The accusation had to be totally false because often when I was lying on the couch and listening to every single word that was being spoken—and I could hear no snoring whatsoever—nevertheless, someone in my family would say, "Wake Dad up, he's snoring again." *It's a conspiracy!* I thought.

On Thanksgiving night, my daughter snuck into my bedroom after I had gone to sleep and turned on a tape recorder. The next morning I saw the recorder sitting on the bedside table, rewound the tape, and this is the message she had recorded at the beginning of the tape: "Today is November 23, 1995, and this is a recording of John K. Graham while he is sleeping." She said it like there was something sinister about my sleeping. Then she said, "You will hear intermittent periods of silence, but don't be deceived; he snores!"

For all her efforts, what did Cathey record? Forty-five minutes of dead silence. Not a single snore! Not one. All week long I played the tape to everyone who came by the house. I wanted them to know the burden I had to endure, the untold "abuse" I suffered at the hands of my very own children.

However, snoring or no snoring, I was asleep, wasn't I? In fact, I was dead asleep. And that's what the reading from Matthew's Gospel is all about. Jesus said that we are a people who are sound asleep and not aware the hour is late, the final day at hand. In every generation, God has raised up men and women who have cried out to awaken people from their slumber. Whenever the prophets of old experienced poverty, injustice, and oppression, they appeared on the streets of Jerusalem, lamenting and seeking to arouse God's people. Usually, the response from the public was to avoid listening and to try to shut the messenger up. What disturbs me is that every now and then, a situation will cause me to suddenly realize I have been asleep and didn't even know it.

Recently, I heard someone identify another person's comments as being racist and what struck me was that I had not even realized it. For years I have prided myself on not being racist, and then I discovered I am still dealing with the problem. I am asleep, and I didn't even know it. In a hundred other ways, you and I are asleep. Unaware of our personal and corporate sin, we add to the problem, and, because we live in denial, all too often we hurt those we love the most.

Jesus said this is like the day of Noah, before the flood, when people were going their merry way—eating and drinking, marrying and giving in marriage—right up to the day when the flood came and they were washed away. And Jesus said so it will be at the coming of the Son of Man. People will be eating and drinking, marrying and giving in marriage—right up to the day when Christ will return, like people in the day of Noah, who did not listen to the prophets of their day. Day after day, Noah and his sons built the ark, telling everyone about the flood that was to come, but no one listened. They only mocked and made fun of Noah and his family.

Jesus used another analogy. He said if the members of the household had known the hour the thief would be coming, they would have stayed on the watch and would not have let the house be broken into. How about you? Have you ever had your home broken into? Statistically, many of us will have that experience this year or in our lifetime. When we least expect it, our homes will be robbed and our possessions stolen.

Pat and I once had things stolen from our home. Day after day we found new items missing. Among them were Pat's original settings for her wedding and engagement rings. Next, Pat's sorority pin and my fraternity pin disappeared. This particularly upset Pat, because she had planned to have the two pins put together in a frame. We were "pinned" to each other before we were married, you see. Next, Pat discovered that five Kennedy mint coin sets had disappeared—she had saved one for each of our children. Then a collection of silver dollars she had planned to give the children was gone.

As if that weren't enough, one Saturday morning when we were away, our then-thirteen-year-old daughter Cathey was startled to find a man standing in the entrance to our home. She asked, "What are you doing here?" The man said he had come to ask for a job. To which she said something that sent chills up our spine when we heard it. She told the man, "You had better leave. I am all alone, and my Dad would be very mad if he knew you were here." Thankfully, the man left. What followed was a thorough parental instruction to our children never to tell an intruder they are alone!

What a frightening experience—having the sacred space of your home violated. But, to be completely honest, I have a confession to make. Having my wife's irreplaceable items stolen did not "awaken" me. I hated that they were gone, to be sure, but it didn't awaken me. You see, these items were precious to Pat, not me. I discounted their value and told Pat she shouldn't be so attached to worldly possessions. I even quoted the Sermon on the Mount to her, trying to tell her these were the kinds of things that moth and rust corrupt, that thieves break in and steal. I reminded her to put her trust in God, not in earthly things.

Oh, I was altogether "wonderful." Even having an intruder confront my daughter didn't awaken me. I reasoned that angels were guarding our children, so why should we worry?

I was very much asleep to what was happening until something very precious to me was stolen. I'll never forget the day I walked into the kitchen, threw together a sandwich to eat, and then prepared to watch the midday news. Then, to my shock, I discovered that my precious black-and-white, portable TV with the four-inch screen had disappeared. I almost fainted. How could it happen! I loved that little TV—my favorite possession, stolen right before my very eyes.

That did it! The thief had stolen my most precious thing. Immediately I sprang into action and called a security service. Before the week was out, our entire building was secured. You couldn't open a window or door anywhere without setting off an alarm. Motion detectors could pick up the slightest movement, night or day. I even began researching putting in security cameras to monitor the grounds—like the home of a celebrity or an important diplomat.

All this time Pat had been quietly watching me spring into action, crawling all over the house, making sure not a single entry point had been missed. Then one day she softly called to my attention the fact that I had not responded when her jewelry was stolen, and I had not responded when our daughter was confronted by an intruder. Instead, what had gotten my attention was when my little four-inch TV was stolen. At first I tried to protest, but finally I had to admit that she was right. It hurt to realize the depth of my sin—my blindness to what was of value to my wife.

What does it take to awaken me from my slumber? I'll tell you what it takes—just touch something that is important to me. And I suspect that you are not too different from me. I suspect we all are dead asleep in some area of our life—snoring at 100 decibels, unaware of what is happening.

As it turned out, Cathey was right after all: I *do* snore. I think I always knew it, but always there was a doubt in my mind, at least to some extent. The night before we left town, Cathey succeeded. For the third night in a row she recorded forty-five minutes of my sleep. Only, this time, she got it on tape. Oh, was I snoring! I was sawing wood with the best of them. No doubt about it. I couldn't deny it any longer. She had the proof.

Snoring can disturb a household. Even worse is to be *spiritually* asleep. We may have been spiritually awake in the past, but now we have fallen asleep. We no longer pray and seek God's will for our life, no longer give to others in the way we once did. The world can be falling apart all around us. Our children are being devoured, and we are sound asleep. We are not living as we ought to, and we know it. So, God sends the wake-up call. Often this means that God will allow that precious thing in our life to be touched. Sometimes, nothing else can awaken the one who is asleep. Why is that? Because spiritual slumber is not like a person who has physically gone to sleep. In physical sleep, we awaken automatically after a few hours of rest. This is not true for spiritual slumber; we will remain asleep forever unless God awakens us.

And God does try to awaken us. God speaks to us most clearly from his Word, the Bible, if we will listen. How clearer can God speak than through Scripture, where we are exhorted to "lay aside the works of darkness and put on the armor of light" (Romans 13:12)? What are the works of darkness? Paul gives us a list, as if we needed reminding. We are not to spend our time in reveling and drunkenness, not in debauchery and licentiousness, not in quarreling and jealousy. Instead, much like a coat, we are to put on Jesus Christ and "make no provision for the flesh, to gratify its desires" (13:14).

I don't know about you, but for me, just being told the right thing to do doesn't help. I can hear Paul's admonition not to engage in debauchery and licentiousness, not to quarrel or be jealous, nor to make provision for the lusts of the flesh; I know I am to put on the Lord Jesus Christ, but doing it is another thing. Why is that? Because I am asleep spiritually, but my flesh is awake. My sinful human nature is all too alive. This means I need salvation in these areas of my life. My soul may be secure eternally, but I have not yet "let go and let God" in these areas of my life. My ego is still in control, and that is why I need God to awaken me from my slumber.

Come, Lord, and do what only you can do—awaken me from my slumber!

Chapter 18

Michael Crichton, Authenticity, and The Authentic One

Then Pilate entered the headquarters again, summoned Jesus, and asked him, "Are you the King of the Jews?" Jesus answered, "Do you ask this on your own, or did others tell you about me?" Pilate replied, "I am not a Jew, am I? Your own nation and the chief priests have handed you over to me. What have you done?" Jesus answered, "My kingdom is not from this world. If my kingdom were from this world, my followers would be fighting to keep me from being handed over to the Jews. But as it is, my kingdom is not from here." Pilate asked him, "So you are a king?" Jesus answered, "You say that I am a king. For this I was born, and for this I came into the world, to testify to the truth. Everyone who belongs to the truth listens to my voice." Pilate asked him, "What is truth?" After he had said this, he went out to the Jews again and told them, "I find no case against him." (John 18:33-38)

*I*n 2000, we had all five of our children and ten grandchildren with us for the Thanksgiving holidays. It made for a most interesting week. On that Sunday, following our morning services, I arrived thirty minutes after our family had gathered at a nearby restaurant. When Graham Knight, who was three years of age, saw me take my seat and noticed that there was no tableware at my place, he said, "Don't worry, Dr. Buddy [his nickname for me], they will bring you a place mat and crayons." Children have a way of bringing us down to earth and setting things right, don't they?

The book of Revelation means to set things right, too. It says that Jesus Christ is "the faithful witness, the firstborn of the dead, and the ruler of the kings of the earth" (1:5). This means that those in this present age who appear to set the rules and those who appear to control the destiny of nations—all will one day be rendered silent by Jesus Christ, who is ultimately the Alpha and the Omega, the beginning and the end, the Lord God Almighty. He is King of kings and Lord of lords.

Michael Crichton is one of my favorite novelists. In his book *Timeline,* he has one of the characters ask, "What is the dominant mode of experience at the end of the twentieth century? How do people view things and what are their expectations?" Answering his own question, the character says, "In every field, from business to politics to marketing to education, the dominant mode has become entertainment. Today everyone expects to be entertained, and they expect to be entertained all the time. Business meetings must be snappy, with bullet lists and animated graphics, so executives aren't bored."

Crichton goes on to say that "malls and stores must be engaging, so as to amuse as well as sell. Politicians must have pleasing video personalities and tell us only what we want to hear. Schools must be careful not to bore young minds that expect the speed of computers and the complexity of television programming. Everyone must be entertained. This is the reality of Western society at the end of the century."[1]

Although I agree with Crichton, I don't think this is altogether a bad thing. Seems to me that's just where we are, and it's the natural product of a people raised with the Internet and Nintendos. People enjoy being entertained, and I admit that I do. I went to see the Disney on Ice production of *Beauty and the Beast* along with my children and grandchildren. We were thoroughly entertained, and that was perfectly fine with me. My reasoning would not satisfy Michael Crichton, who laments that in other centuries, "human beings wanted to be saved, or improved, or freed, or educated, but in our day we want to be entertained."[2] He says that our great fear is not of disease or death but boredom.

When will our mania for entertainment end? Crichton says that sooner or later, the artificiality of entertainment will become unbearable, and when that happens, he believes it will cause people to seek authenticity. And what is *authentic?* He says it is "anything that is not devised and structured. Anything that is not controlled by other people. Anything that exists for its own sake. Anything that assumes its own shape is authentic."[3]

---

1. Michael Crichton, *Timeline.* (New York: Alfred A. Knopf, 1999), p. 400.
2. Ibid., p. 401.
3. Ibid., p. 401.

This search for authenticity provides the setting for Crichton's book. He asks, "Where will people turn in the twenty-first century for the rare and desirable experience of authenticity?" Crichton says that they will turn to the past. "The past alone is authentic. It is the world that existed before Disney and Murdoch and Nissan and Sony and IBM and all the other shapers of the present day. And people will want to travel into the past in order to have an authentic experience." In the book, this quest causes scientists to build a quantum time-travel machine that can transport a person to parallel universes where he or she can truly experience authentic past events.

On Thanksgiving afternoon, 2000, after being stuffed with a marvelous turkey dinner, I mentioned Crichton's book and asked my family where they would like to go in the past if they could get there in a time machine. My daughter Ginger immediately said, "Can you guarantee that I can return whenever I want to, intact?" My other daughters were just as skeptical, and my wife, Pat, didn't want to go back at all—not to any single day. Clearly the women in my household prefer the here and now.

My elder son finally spoke up. Kirk said he wanted to go back before the November 7, 2000, election and tell George W. Bush to spend more time campaigning in Florida. This prompted my younger son, Patrick, to say he wanted to go back to the day President John F. Kennedy was assassinated to see if there were any gunmen on the grassy knoll in Dallas that day.

When it came my turn, I said I wanted to go back to the first century so I could walk with Jesus. I wanted to see him heal people and hear him give his Sermon on the Mount. I wanted to be with him on the day he died on the cross, and I wanted to be there when he was resurrected from the dead. I wanted to be with Jesus. This prompted Cathey to say, "Dad, of course. Why didn't we think of that?"

Why would I want to go back to see Jesus? Because for me, Jesus is the one who validates everything I do and gives authenticity to my very life and the life of the church that I love.

The feast day of Christ the King, the Sunday before Advent, celebrates the authenticity of Jesus—that he is reliable, credible, genuine, the real thing. Although this feast is relatively recent in origin, having been instituted by Pope Pius XI in 1925, the message it proclaims is not. It is something the church has said for two thousand years—that

Jesus of Nazareth, a first-century Jew who stood trial before Pilate and who died a cruel death on the cross, will one day reign as King of kings and Lord of lords.

Many Christians seem to be uncomfortable with the idea of Jesus being a king. Perhaps this is because we do not like the idea of anyone ruling over us—not even Jesus. Yet, the intensity of our presidential election campaigns emphasizes that we all know how important it is who will be our top leader. The person we elect President affects the course of this nation for decades to come. Yes, it is vitally important who we elect as our leaders, and that's why we want a President who is a person of integrity, one who has the wisdom to lead wisely, and one who cares about all the people, not just his people. Above all, I think we want a President who will serve as a role model for our children and for us, too.

Yet as important as the election of the President of our nation is, there is One, as we are told in John 18, who is even greater. There is One who is rightly called a king and yet is not like any ordinary king—not a king who sits on a throne with servants kneeling at his feet. Instead, in John's Gospel we find King Jesus on trial for his life. He is on the way to the cross and certain death.

Pilate asked, "Are you the King of the Jews?" Jesus answered, "My kingdom is not from this world." Here was a king like no one had ever seen. The people in Jesus' day wanted a king like King David. They wanted a king who would lead them with a sword, who would cut down their enemies.

But Jesus did not come with the power of a sword; he came with the power of love. He did not rule from a throne, but from a cross. He did not ride in a chariot; he rode on the back of a donkey. He did not cater to the powerful; Jesus was with the sick and ate with the outcasts of society.

No wonder Jesus failed by earthly standards. He was arrested, mocked, whipped, and forced to carry his own cross down the *Via Dolorosa* ("Way of Sorrows") to Golgotha. Within hours, the King of the Jews was dead. And that should be the end of the story. A babe was born in Bethlehem, grew up, did some nice things for people, but died at age thirty-three. End of story. Period.

Only, that *wasn't* the end of Jesus' story, was it? Three days later, God raised him from the dead. And as we find ourselves in the third millennium, some 2,000 years after the birth of Christ, hundreds of millions of men and women are breaking bread and drinking wine on Sunday, proclaiming they are disciples of King Jesus.

What about those who killed Jesus? Where are they? They are gone! Where are our Lord's accusers? They are gone! Where is Herod? Gone! Where are the Roman soldiers? They are gone! Where is the Roman Empire? It too is gone!

In this amazing turn of events, the most powerful people in Jesus' day have turned to dust. But the one they killed lives on—not only in heaven, but also in the hearts of countless disciples around the globe. I don't know about you, but the longer I know Jesus, the more I love him and the happier I am to be called his disciple. That's why the authentic is found in Jesus Christ and why everything else pales in comparison. Jesus was "the real thing" in the first century, and he is the real thing today as well.

Want to know what is *authenticity?* Authenticity is my three-year-old grandson telling me not to worry—that they will bring me a place mat and crayons. And authenticity is Jesus Christ going to the cross to die for the sins of the whole world.

Michael Crichton says the authentic person is the person who is not devised, structured, or controlled by other people. The authentic makes its own shape. I can't think of a better description of Jesus. He was not controlled or shaped by anyone except his heavenly Father. No one could shape Jesus' character; instead, Jesus molds and shapes all who follow him and make him their Lord and Savior.

The more I think about it, the more certain I am that we don't need a time machine to find authenticity, nor do we need to go back to the first century to find Jesus. We can walk with him right now because he has promised to be with us. The most authentic person who ever lived is Jesus Christ, and that's why we who believe proclaim so loudly, "Christ is King!" Yes, Christ is King, indeed!

Chapter 19

I Was Taught to Doubt

But Thomas (who was called the Twin), one of the twelve, was not with them when Jesus came. So the other disciples told him, "We have seen the Lord." But he said to them, "Unless I see the mark of the nails in his hands, and put my finger in the mark of the nails and my hand in his side, I will not believe." A week later his disciples were again in the house, and Thomas was with them. Although the doors were shut, Jesus came and stood among them and said, "Peace be with you." Then he said to Thomas, "Put your finger here and see my hands. Reach out your hand and put it in my side. Do not doubt but believe." Thomas answered him, "My Lord and my God!" Jesus said to him, "Have you believed because you have seen me? Blessed are those who have not seen and yet have come to believe." (John 20:24-29)

During my medical training I was often involved in research. Several years ago, while studying John's Gospel it occurred to me that as a medical student I had been thoroughly trained to doubt, to be a "Doubting Thomas."

I recalled sitting in meetings in the department of physiology at Tulane Medical School, where members of the staff would present their projects. First, researchers would state the hypothesis they hoped to prove or disprove. After stating the hypothesis, they would give a step-by-step description of how the study had been carried out. Next, they would enumerate the results of the study, give a statistical analysis, and, finally, state the conclusions. Then, the entire team would play the devil's advocate and attempt to find flaws in either the method or the calculations—we would doubt the conclusion, if you will. We also discussed the strengths of the study, as well as its weaknesses. This creative flow of ideas was very exciting to me.

In those meetings, two different kinds of doubt were modeled for me. The first kind of doubt was not healthy—it was the stubborn refusal to believe. No matter what facts were presented, you could never have enough proof to convince these people. They are the true cynics of life and often die with their skepticism.

There was a second kind of doubt—a healthy doubt. I would call it a searching doubt—a doubt that wants to believe—a doubt that yearns for the hypothesis to be true, but at the same time has the courage to say, "Unless you can bring me the facts, unless I can see the hard data with my own eyes, I will not believe." The important thing that makes this kind of doubt good is that when the results of a project are convincing, this person can celebrate that fact. I believe Thomas had this kind of doubt, a healthy doubt that yearns for the hypothesis to be true.

"We have seen the Lord!" the disciples exclaimed. Then the other disciples proclaimed their hypothesis: "He is risen!" Thomas was startled. He had not been present with the other disciples. "Risen? The Lord? But, he is dead." With all the integrity of any good scientist, Thomas declared, "Unless I see the mark of the nails in his hands, and put my finger in the mark of the nails and my hand in his side, I will not believe."

A week passed. Once again, the disciples were behind locked doors, except this time Thomas was with them. Now, with all eleven of the disciples present (Judas Iscariot was no longer a disciple by this time), Jesus appeared and stood in their midst. In my mind's eye, I can see Jesus and Thomas standing there—looking at each another. God the Son confronting man, and man face-to-face with the Son of God. Thomas was afraid, yet he wanted to believe.

Finally Jesus spoke, "Thomas, look at my hands. Reach out your finger and put it into the mark of the nails." Thomas stood frozen, unable to utter a word, unable to move. Jesus was persistent, "Thomas, reach your hand here, and put it into my side. Do not be unbelieving, but believe." Immediately, Thomas fell to his knees and exclaimed, "My Lord and my God!" Saying this, Thomas made the greatest confession about Jesus in the entire New Testament and accorded Jesus the recognition of deity. Thomas was saying, "Jesus, you are the God of Abraham, Isaac, and Jacob. Jesus, you are *Yahweh,* the God of Israel." Quite a confession for any Jew to make.

After Thomas had made his remarkable confession, Jesus said this: "Have you believed because you have seen me? Blessed are those who have not seen and yet have come to believe" (John 20:29). Christ's blessing was given to those who have no such experience as Thomas and yet who believe. To be human is to doubt. Healthy doubt, like Thomas, will fall to its knees and say, "My Lord and my God!"

Several years ago, shortly after I was ordained a deacon and it still felt very strange to wear a clerical collar around my neck, a parishioner at St. Matthew's in Austin, invited my wife, Pat, and me to join her for dinner at a restaurant on the top floor of the tallest building in Austin. The featured speaker that night was an aerospace engineer from NASA, Dr. Hans Mark, who had been very instrumental in the development of the space shuttle program. Since I was a boy, I always loved anything to do with space and looked forward to the talk.

Pat helped me dress as I struggled to put on my finest for the occasion—a new black suit, a Graham-tartan rabat, white collar, cuff links, and silver cross. I looked wonderful! At the restaurant, our attendant ushered Pat and me to one of the few tables that still had vacant seats. First we heard the lecture on the space program, and then we went through the buffet line and returned to our seats for dinner.

We had hardly settled in our seats when a man around sixty-five years old sitting at the table with us, recognizing that I was a man of the cloth, looked me straight in the eye and declared, "I am not a man of faith. I have a lot of doubts, and I certainly don't believe all that stuff in the New Testament about Jesus." That's how he began our conversation.

I swallowed hard and said, "Well, sir, first let me say, you are correct to be cautious about what the New Testament says concerning Jesus Christ, because it says he was not just a man, it says Jesus was God Incarnate, and that should cause you to pause. But, when you say you have many doubts, I think you assume that means you are not a believer. Actually, I define doubt as 'faith struggling to believe.' To me, you are a man of faith who is struggling to believe. Otherwise, you wouldn't even have brought up the name of Jesus in our conversation."

This was the beginning of a thirty-minute conversation in which the two of us took hardly a bite to eat. I was riveted by this man, and he was riveted by me. No one else at the table said a single word. They just ate quietly, not daring to interrupt what was obviously one of those God-arranged moments in time.

After about thirty minutes of us bantering back and forth, I suddenly knew what I should say to this man. I paused for a moment and said,

"Sir, this is not the first time you have had this conversation, is it?" He said, "No. It isn't." I said, "In fact, you have had this conversation many times in your life, haven't you?" He said that was true. I continued, "And always, you have left these kinds of conversations more certain you are not a believer, isn't that true?" He agreed, and I said, "Sir, you know it was no accident we sat at this table, don't you?" He said, "I don't believe in accidents."

At this point the woman who had invited us to the dinner, a friend, interrupted our conversation and tried to give a spiritual interpretation as to what was happening. She said, "Ever since the two of you began talking, have you noticed all the birds that have been flying all around outside our window?"

"Probably an updraft," the man declared.

I said, "Yes sir, I am sure you are right. There probably is an updraft outside this building, but I believe my friend wants us to know that something profoundly spiritual is taking place."

I then said, "Sir, you do know why we are having this conversation, don't you?" He said, "No, why?" I said, "The reason I am sitting at this table and we are having this conversation is because God loves you very much, and God won't let you go. You have been afraid to accept Christ's love, but God hasn't rejected you. God loves you."

At this, the man began to weep, and, embarrassed, he stood up, grabbed his wife by the arm, and said, "Let's go." And off they went. The other couple who had been sitting with us was in shock, and the man said, "We are Christians, and we have never seen anything like that in our entire life. It was wonderful!"

The very next Sunday, the wife of the man with whom I had had the dinner conversation showed up at St. Matthew's, but her husband was not with her. She told me that he said he would never go to church. I wrote him numerous letters and notes, and sent him books to read, but he always told his wife he was not going to come to church.

I continued to pray for him daily. Several months passed. Suddenly I felt inspired to write one more time, and I knew what I was to say. I wrote, "Sir, from our many conversations I can see that you are a man of great intelligence, but what I don't know is whether you are a man of courage. If you are, I challenge you to attend just one worship service."

The next Sunday morning, as I processed down the aisle, I saw that he was present and, as we sang high praise to God, tears were streaming down his cheeks. A few days later he called me to say that he had never been baptized, and he wanted me to baptize him. What a joy it was for me to baptize this dear man, pour water on his head in the name of the Father, Son, and Holy Spirit, mark the sign of the cross on his forehead, and say, "You are marked as Christ's own forever." When I finished, tears were streaming down all our cheeks.

Within weeks, he began attending my confirmation class, and a few months later he was confirmed. Every Sunday after that he came to church, and always tears were streaming down his face when he knelt to take Holy Communion.

The fact is, what this man needed was someone to help him realize that his doubts were actually his faith struggling to believe. Once he saw that to be true, he joyfully accepted Jesus Christ as his personal Lord and Savior.

Many people have doubts. They have doubts about God, doubts about the Resurrection, doubts about Jesus Christ, doubts about the people who profess faith in him, and doubts about the church. For those who struggle with doubt, I have two things to tell them.

First, I say they could have been on my medical research team any day—they have the critical mind we needed.

Second, I want them to know they could be a part of my church. We are all in the process of coming to know more perfectly what it means to love God. No one has arrived at perfect knowledge of God, and certainly not me. We are all in process.

Third, I pray that they will not let their doubts hinder them any longer. Instead, I invite them to let their doubt be the proof that they indeed are a man or woman of faith—one who is struggling to believe, but is, nevertheless, a person of faith. I believe that the reason we struggle to believe is that we only want to profess what we know to be absolutely true. I salute that attitude, and at the same time I invite all who doubt to open their hearts to the One who has demonstrated he loves us, God as revealed in Jesus Christ.

Finally, I invite them to give their doubts to God and to give themselves to Jesus Christ. Like the disciple Thomas, say, "My Lord and my God." Do this, and we are counted among those who are blessed of God because though we have not seen, yet we have believed.

Chapter 20

My Train Set, Lienhard's Engines
of Our Ingenuity, and Forgiveness

Then Peter came and said to him, "Lord, if another member of the
church sins against me, how often should I forgive? As many as
seven times?" Jesus said to him, "Not seven times, but, I tell you,
seventy-seven times." (Matthew 18:21-22)

*J*ohn Lienhard is the M. D. Anderson Professor of Mechanical
Engineering and History at the University of Houston. He has a fascinating program that I listen to often. It is called *The Engines of Our*
Ingenuity and is heard daily over National Public Radio. Lienhard has
recently published a book by the same name, and in his book he says
that the story of humanity is also the story of the machines and objects
that become a part of our lives from the day we are born until the day
we die. We have a symbiotic relationship with the automobiles we
drive, with computers that talk back to us, with the homes in which we
live, and with the churches in which we worship. So interwoven is
human history with the history of technology, Lienhard says, that the
best name for our species is not *Homo sapiens* (which means "wise
being"), the best name for our species is *Homo technologicus:* We are
the species that creates technology, and in turn, we are transformed by
the tools and structures we make.

I have thought a lot about Lienhard's concept, and I believe his thesis
is not limited to technology. It applies to every area of life, including
music, the arts, literature, and religion. This is not to say that everything
we create is good. The "ideas" we create can become the engines that
separate us into warring camps, and this isn't because the ideas we
hold are true.

The truth is, because we are finite beings, the ideas we create are approximations of the truth, at best, and never the whole truth. The problem is that we believe our ideas are the *whole* truth, and that is why the engines of our ingenuity can quickly lead us down the primrose path to division and strife. When other people do not accept our view of things, we become bitter, angry, and resentful. If this takes place in marriage, we may file for divorce. If our problem is in the church, we may look for another one. When one nation is pitted against another, we go to war and people die. This is true of every area of life, including our relationship with God, our marriages, and our churches, and it is the fuel for bitterness and strife, where unforgiveness rules the day.

The Reverend John Yates is the rector of The Falls Church (Episcopal) in Falls Church, Virginia. In 2000, he spoke to the men of St. Martin's in Houston and began his talk by saying that several years before, he had spoken to the same men's group on the subject of forgiveness. Yates said the talk he gave was one of his most brilliant messages. He addressed the problem of unforgiveness and explained point by point exactly how a person could forgive anyone of anything, no matter how painful the situation. When he finished his talk, he said, he sat down feeling quite proud of himself, only to have the man sitting next to him shake his head and say, "Forgiveness ain't that easy."

The problem is, we think that if we forgive someone, that means we must approve or sanction the actions of the person who harmed us. This is not true. Forgiveness does not mean that we must accept abusive behavior and have no boundaries in life. Nor does forgiveness mean the offending person is to be released from the consequences of his or her actions. Quite the contrary; a just society will demand sanctions for unacceptable behavior, and an effective judicial system is important if we are to live together in civility. Forgiveness is not talking about what needs to happen to the other person. Forgiveness is about how we deal with the pain in our own lives.

Yet, so few people have learned to forgive. Instead, it is as if we are riding on a train headed to destruction, blowing our whistle, tooting our horn, ranting and raving, dividing into camps, and, in many cases, both sides absolutely certain God is on their side.

Dr. Carla Cooper serves as executive director of St. Luke's Episcopal Health Charities at St. Luke's Hospital in Houston. Carla described a trip she took to Northern Ireland this way:

My first glimpse of Ireland was magnificent—it was a rolling pano-
rama of vivid green hills and fields right out of a sentimental Irish
storybook. There were small herds of brilliant white sheep grazing by
hedgerows and little cottages. It was pastoral, peaceful, timeless—
a beatific vision of life. A short while later, as we approached the city's
center, I thought I was back in Texas. New buildings, office towers, a
sparkling convention center, lots of hotels, restaurants, and shops—all
signs of a prosperous and booming economy. As we continued, we
arrived in the "real" Belfast, the Belfast of the Troubles, the Belfast of
two worlds—vast neighborhoods of grim little Protestant houses and
shops on one side and grim little Catholic houses and shops on the
other. And right down the middle is a HUGE two to three story wall.
Each side looked exactly the same—ugly, hard, poor. This wasn't just
because the neighborhoods were poor and there were virtually no trees
or grass, but because it was a landscape transformed by and organized
around the darkest of human qualities: hatred and fear. Everywhere on
the sides of buildings were the expressions of anger and revenge. Huge
paintings of martyrs to the respective causes, clenched fists, guns,
chains, huge paintings of black hooded paramilitaries waving weapons
in righteous anger, standing at the foot of graves, graves more often
than not depicted as still bleeding. To me this wall is the emblem of
all the intractable conflict and violence in the world. It was the embodi-
ment of that peculiar capacity of human beings to turn their neighbors
into "the other," (people who are) not just unlike me in every way, but
against me in every way—beyond forgiveness, beyond redemption,
even into the grave.[1]

An acquaintance recently asked me if I had ever experienced prejudice. He went on to say that during a recent trip to Scotland, when he
signed the register in a small hotel the owner said, "You are not welcome here." My acquaintance said, "Why not, aren't we dressed nice
enough? Isn't my money good enough?" To which the innkeeper
replied, "You are a Campbell, and your people killed, raped, and plun-
dered my people four hundred years ago. No Campbell will ever spend
a night under my roof."

---

1. Carla Cooper, "Reflections on Belfast: Meditation as a Way of Peace." Spirituality
and Health Series Lecture given at Palmer Memorial Episcopal Church in Houston,
February 14, 2001.

Absurd? Hard to believe in this day and age? Absolutely, but the fact is, we humans have the capacity to turn our loved ones, our best friends, our neighbors, and even perfect strangers into people who are beyond forgiveness, beyond redemption, to the grave, as Dr. Cooper attested, yet even beyond. From Bosnia to Rwanda to Ceylon and the United States of America—virtually every nation on earth can affirm this to be true. Unforgiveness is a human problem that none can escape. It is present among Christians too. It doesn't help even for us to know that Jesus taught his disciples to ask God to forgive our sins according to the same measure that we are willing to forgive those who have sinned against us. We tell God that we forgive our enemies, but our smoldering anger and resentment declare we *haven't* forgiven, not really.

When I was a boy, I received a train set for Christmas. I loved that train and played with it all day long. My parents knew I loved to draw pictures of logging trucks, so they bought me a train car that carried logs. I could stop the train and dump the logs onto a side platform. I must have dumped those logs a thousand times. After a few weeks, the oval-shaped track became boring. My engine could only go around in circles.

Unforgiveness is like my model train set—it keeps us going around in circles and getting nowhere. Often, we refuse to forgive the person who has harmed us because we think that if we forgive them, we are condoning their behavior. The only problem is, we are the ones who suffer the most. The other person probably isn't even thinking about us, but all we can think about is them and what they did to us. What has happened is that our unforgiveness has stuck us to our painful past, and, like superglue, it won't let go. The engine of our ingenuity keeps on chugging along, 'round and 'round in circles, again and again, always returning to the same old dumping ground. It is so hard to realize that we are the ones who are suffering, because the engine on which we have chosen to ride continually fuels our anger and bitterness.

John Lienhard believes that historians are inaccurate when they describe the medieval period as being "the Dark Ages," a time when there was little technological advancement. He says that if we look most carefully, we will find that medieval Europe was a very creative period, and the prime example he gives is the creation of the gothic cathedrals during that era. In one of his talks on cathedrals, Lienhard quotes historian and novelist H. G. Wells, who said that societies take on two forms: they are either "communities of the will" or they are "communities of obedience." Because ancient Israel was rightly committed to God, it was a community of the will, according to Wells. By communities of obedience Wells means submission, and he gave the medieval church as an example. By submitting themselves to God, who worked through them, Wells said they were able to create miracles. And that they did. Consider one twelfth-century witness's comments about France's Chartres Cathedral, and you'll see what Wells meant:

> When the towers seemed to be rising as if by magic, the faithful harnessed themselves to the carts and dragged them from the quarry to the cathedral. The enthusiasm spread throughout France. Men and women came from far away carrying provisions for the workmen—wine, oil, corn. Among them were lords and ladies, pulling carts with the rest. There was perfect discipline and a most profound silence. All hearts were united and each man forgave his enemies.[2]

"Each man forgave his enemies." How do we forgive *our* enemies? How do we forgive those who have hurt us deeply? I believe that we can find a clue by reading the liturgy of the Burial Office, the most powerful service in the *Book of Common Prayer*. In that service we ask God to "help us, we pray, in the midst of things we cannot understand, to believe and trust in the communion of saints, the forgiveness of sins, and the resurrection to life everlasting. Amen."[3]

The prayer tells us five things that can help break the demonic cycle that ensnares our hearts and souls when we find it impossible to forgive those who have hurt us.

(1) First, we need to ask for God's help, acknowledging that we can't do this alone. (2) The *Book of Common Prayer* recognizes that we are in the midst of things we cannot understand this side of heaven. (3) The third thing is to "believe and trust in the communion of saints." (4) The fourth thing our prayer book says is that we are to believe and trust in the forgiveness of sins—that God was in Christ reconciling the world

---

2. John Lienhard, *(The Engines of Our Ingenuity.* New York: Oxford University Press, 2000), p. 22.

3. *The Book of Common Prayer.* (New York: Church Hymnal Corporation, 1979), p. 481.

unto himself. (5) The final thing this prayer has to say about forgiveness is that we are to "trust in the resurrection to life everlasting." I believe we can never truly forgive a person who has hurt us deeply without seeing things from God's perspective—without having an eternal view of things.

If John Lienhard is right when he says that we are the technology we create, and if I am right when I say we are the ideas we create—that our ideas become the engines that fuel our ingenuity, causing us to behave the way we do—then I want to paint another picture for you to hold alongside the picture of that wall in Belfast, Ireland. That wall represents hatred, anger, revenge and unforgiveness. The other picture I want to describe is a wall in Oklahoma City, built following the 1995 tragedy of the bombing of the Alfred P. Murrah Federal Building.

In the summer of 1999, my wife and I visited good friends in Oklahoma City who took us to see the site of the explosion. What was left of the building had been demolished. What remained was a cyclone wire fence that had been erected to keep people away from the bombing site. On that wire fence people had begun to pour out their hearts and express their grief. They did so by hanging pictures of their loved ones, often decorated lavishly with ribbons and flowers. They wrote poems to express how much their loved ones were missed. There were family pictures and pictures of the churches of which the departed had been a member. Notes were stuck all along the wire fence. Some were written by children to their mother or father who was killed, to say how much they missed them. Scripture verses were everywhere. Groups from around the world—firefighters, police officers, and members of the armed services—all had sent letters. Vietnam veterans had hung a sign to say they joined with the families in their grief. Hundreds of people lined the fence, and what struck me was the profound silence. If anyone spoke, it was softly and in whispers. Most said hardly a word. Many wiped tears from their eyes. Everyone was touched by this amazing outpouring of love from around the world. People had lost those most precious to them, yet in their grief they were surrounded by the community of the saints, and the sense of eternity and the presence of God was everywhere.

Two fences: one in Belfast, Ireland, representing hatred and revenge, dividing and separating two peoples, both claiming to be Christian; another wall—this one in Oklahoma City—representing love and the unity of people from around the world. Just to see that wall was a healing experience. You could sense that God was there.

As I have thought about these two walls, I have to wonder. What kind of walls have I been building in my life? Walls of hatred or of love? The fact is, we have a choice when we are hurt and abused, maligned and rejected. We can turn against the other person in anger; but when we do that, we only hurt ourselves and bind ourselves to them. Instead, God invites us to build a wall of love, to hang ribbons and write poems to tell those who hurt us that we still love them and forgive them.

Perhaps we should all erect a cyclone fence—or draw a picture of one—a wall to represent the places of loss and pain in our lives. We could hang cards and letters there, write verses of Scripture, and notes to say that one day we will be together in God's heaven, and all this will be past. Build a wall of love, and we will begin the process of healing our pain, free to enter, unencumbered, the future that God has for us. Unforgiveness will hold us like superglue to the hurtful experiences of our past and keep us going around in circles. Forgiveness is the solvent that can set us free.

When I was a boy, I loved to go to the Louisiana State Fair. Once a year I got to see the largest model train set I could ever imagine. It had five different tracks with trains of every description heading in every direction. There were mountains, valleys, rivers, and streams. There were towns dotting the hillsides, with church steeples rising into the sky. And none of the tracks were mere circles—all had switches, so there were many alternatives. The engineer could send a train for a long trip through a valley, or by turning another switch it would disappear into a long tunnel before finally emerging on the other side of the mountain. Every year when we went to the state fair, I would stand for hours watching those trains. No other exhibit held the fascination for me that this one did. I think what sparked my imagination was the fact that these trains offered endless possibilities.

Forgiveness is like that. It sets us free so that we don't always go to the same dumping place. Forgiveness is an invitation from God. Forgiveness is the way to be healed from our past wounds. Forgiveness is the way to be set free. It may not be easy, but forgiveness is God's way, and it works.

Wells made a distinction between two forms of society—communities of will and communities of obedience. I believe that God has called us to be both, to be a community of will and a community of obedience. A "community of will" because of the depth of the commitment we must make if we are going to truly forgive those who have hurt us, and a "community of obedience" because it is God who has said that we will be forgiven of our sins exactly to the measure we forgive those who sin against us. And, like the people who built gothic cathedrals long ago, when we forgive we will have tasted of the elixir of love and power that comes from the One who said on the cross, "Father, forgive them, for they know not what they do."

Chapter 21

Dr. Rigby's Kaleidoscope and Holy Week

When they had come near Jerusalem and had reached Bethphage, at the Mount of Olives, Jesus sent two disciples, saying to them, "Go into the village ahead of you, and immediately you will find a donkey tied, and a colt with her; untie them and bring them to me. If anyone says anything to you, just say this, 'The Lord needs them.' And he will send them immediately." This took place to fulfill what had been spoken through the prophet, saying, "Tell the daughter of Zion, Look, your king is coming to you, humble, and mounted on a donkey, and on a colt, the foal of a donkey." The disciples went and did as Jesus had directed them; they brought the donkey and the colt, and put their cloaks on them, and he sat on them. A very large crowd spread their cloaks on the road, and others cut branches from the trees and spread them on the road. The crowds that went ahead of him and that followed were shouting, "Hosanna to the Son of David! Blessed is the one who comes in the name of the Lord! Hosanna in the highest heaven!" (Matthew 21:1-9)

As a young boy I loved to go to our family physician's office because in his reception room, he had a wonderful brass kaleidoscope. I loved to turn the scope and watch the endless reshuffling of colors and images. Sometimes the designs were dazzling in beauty, so beautiful I'd share the view with my mother. Other times the combination of colors was dark, drab, and lifeless. When that happened, I always twisted the dial until another bright and cheerful picture filled the screen.

Life is like that, isn't it? One moment we are filled with joy and exhilaration, and the next moment we encounter heart-wrenching pain—pain so intense we wish we could die. At times it seems everyone else is turning the dial of our heart and our emotions are in the hands of another.

Where does our pain come from? Certainly it hurts to lose one's wealth, one's job or position, but surely the most intense pain comes from human relationships. This kind of pain happens when those we love suffer, or when we are rejected—when family and friends suddenly turn the other way, refuse to listen, refuse to let us into their world any longer.

For some, the pain comes from the person who has been a best friend for years. You enjoyed the best of times and the worst of times together. Then, one day your friend stops calling and you don't know why. What hurts the most is that you can't seem to be able to make things right again.

For others, it's your spouse—the person with whom you exchanged vows meant to last a lifetime. Yet, a wall goes up, and you can't reach that person any longer. Someone once put it this way: "I want the person I married back. But that person is gone."

For still others, the pain comes from the child you raised, the very one to whom you gave all you had. Suddenly, they grow up, leave home, and no longer will listen to you. In the process, you feel used, abused, and discarded.

And yet another kind of pain comes from wanting to have children but not being able to give birth, struggling year after year to become pregnant but not being able to conceive or carry to term.

Who can measure this kind of pain—the pain of separation between best of friends, between spouses, between parent and child, or the internal pain that comes from a deep, deep disappointment? Who can measure the pain multiplied a billion times over in the lives of countless people throughout all of human history? Who can measure the pain of simply being human?

I believe Jesus Christ can. Because he was fully human, Jesus can understand what pain is all about. After all, he is the one who said, "Jerusalem, Jerusalem . . . ! How often have I desired to gather your children together as a hen gathers her brood under her wings, and you were not willing!" (Matthew 23:37). A few days later, the people of Jerusalem cried out, "Crucify him! Crucify him!"

It is customary in the Episcopal Church on Palm Sunday for readers and the congregation to join together in recalling the painful events leading up to the crucifixion by presenting a sort of choral reading. The congregation takes the part of the angry crowd, while the readers have assigned roles as Jesus, Herod, Pilate, and others.

You and I crying out on Palm Sunday, "Crucify him! Crucify him!"

I have heard parishioners express alarm at the prospect of saying these words in the Passion liturgy themselves. They say, "I would never be a part of a lynch mob, much less a crowd demanding the death of Jesus. I love Jesus. and it offends me greatly to say these words. These are such violent words, and I am offended by them."

Violent words indeed—*crucify him.* Violent words for a violent act, destroying a person and all that he represents. One thing is for certain, though: At one time or another, we all reject God and all that God represents. If necessary, we will even reject God violently. Sooner or later, following Jesus seems to require too much. Jesus' disciples found this to be true. They followed Jesus every day for three years, as long as there was the hope that something good was going to come to pass. But when they realized following Jesus meant going to the cross with him, they fled—every single one of them. Peter denied Christ three times openly. "I do not know the man!" he said (Matthew 26:74). Can you believe it? One of Jesus' own disciples, one of his closest followers, denying he even knew Jesus?

Let's not kid ourselves. You and I and every single person on earth would have denied Christ before his resurrection. First-century Jewish people did not crucify Jesus; we all did. That is the whole point of Jesus' dying on the cross. He didn't die because the Jews rejected him. No, Christ died for the sin of the whole world. Death on the cross was Jesus' destiny and the purpose for which he was born. The cross was not the greatest mistake of human history; it was the greatest moment in history—the day you and I were cleansed of our sins and made righteous with Christ.

It is only after Jesus was raised from the dead that we can begin to react differently toward him, and I'm not at all sure how differently we would react even knowing Jesus Christ to be the Savior. After all, in the history of the early church, although many were willing to die rather than deny Christ, many more did deny him under the severe persecution of Christians by Roman emperors. That's why the church developed a system of penance to deal with those they called "the lapsed." The lapsed were not just nominal Christians. Many were ordained elders, pastors of local congregations, and some were bishops.

"*I'd* never say, 'Crucify him!'"? I'm not so sure. I think it is wisest for me to know there is a part of me that the apostle Paul called "the flesh," and the fact is, my flesh will do whatever it takes to meet my needs, keep me alive, and keep me in control. My flesh will always reject Jesus Christ and deny his Lordship when the going gets tough.

But although this is true, thankfully God has done the impossible. God has done for us what we could not do. God sent Jesus Christ to go to the cross on our behalf, and on the cross Jesus became the perfect sacrifice and the Lamb of God that takes away the sins of the world. Jesus died for the sins of the whole world. This means that God forgives the sins of every person who seeks his forgiveness.

God did one more thing. God has not left us orphans. God has given us the Holy Spirit. And God's Spirit empowers us to walk the walk, to live no longer after the flesh but according to the Spirit (see Romans 8:3-4). And if we live in the Spirit, Scripture says that we shall be called sons and daughters of God, and our hearts will cry out, "Abba, Father," an Aramaic expression of profound intimacy. It is like referring to God as "Daddy."

The fact is, there is a war going on in my flesh every day of my life, a war in which the forces of evil seek to possess me and draw me away. At the same time, there is the realm of God's Holy Spirit, which seeks to empower me to do God's will, to take up my cross and follow Jesus. That's what Holy Week, the week preceding Easter, is all about—turning from the sin in each of our lives to take up our cross and follow Jesus.

The week begins with a Palm Sunday service, with the "kaleidoscope" turned to visualize the joyful entry into Jerusalem. People are throwing their coats and palm branches into the road and singing, "Hosanna, blessed is he who comes in the name of the Lord!"

Each day in Holy Week the dial of the kaleidoscope is turned one more time and each turn provides yet another view of our Lord's final week on earth. On Monday and Tuesday, Episcopalians come to the church to get before the Lord, to pray and to seek God's face, to confess our sins and the sins of the world. We also come to listen, to listen for that still, small voice of God speaking to our hearts, convicting us of sin, of righteousness, and of judgment.

On Wednesday another scene appears as we gather for a choral *Tenebrae* service. In Latin, *tenebrae* means "darkness" or "shadows." In this service, candles are gradually extinguished until the people sit in darkness and leave in silence.

Thursday evening—Maundy Thursday—the scene changes again, becoming even more darkened. Maundy is a name derived from the ceremony of the washing of the feet, and the Latin words *mandatum novum,* where Jesus said, "A new commandment I give you. " Maundy is the commandment to love. And, so we come to wash each other's feet and watch in silence as the greenery and all decorations are removed from behind the altar rail. Flowers, plants, candlesticks, service books, hymnals, and cushions—everything is removed. The altar is methodically stripped, washed, and left bare. We leave the church in silence.

The kaleidoscope changes again. Now we find ourselves before the Altar of Response. The greenery taken from the church has been brought to the chapel and arranged to depict the garden of Gethsemane, where Jesus said to his disciples, "Could you not pray with me for one hour?" A little later Jesus was arrested and, according to tradition, spent his last night on earth alone in a dark pit that was located in the house of Caiaphas the high priest. We pray before this altar, where a single candle is lighted and is flickering, about to go out. Many spend several hours in prayer, and in many churches an all-night prayer vigil is held. We do this because we have been so touched by God's love that we refuse to let Jesus be alone. We pray all night until noon the next day.

At noon on Good Friday, the kaleidoscope is fixed, and we see only one picture—that of Christ's suffering, his passion on the cross. Many will walk with Jesus down the *Via Dolorosa,* marking each of the fourteen stations of the cross. At each station, we stop, recite prayers, and meditate on the meaning of that particular moment in Jesus' final walk to the cross. Many walk the stations of the cross, and others gather in churches on Good Friday to honor the day Christ died.

In the liturgy for Saturday in Holy Week, we are invited to read the anthem, "In the midst of life," found in the burial office. The brief liturgy brings together the themes and questions it poses, the burial of our Lord, and the Sabbath day of rest. We are invited to ponder prayerfully and with contrite hearts that on this day, Jesus lay in the tomb, dead.

In many of our churches, we return Saturday evening for the Great Vigil of Easter, with Holy Baptism, Confirmation, and the first Holy Eucharist of the Resurrection. The Easter Vigil begins with the lighting of the Paschal candle and the procession in which the celebrant sings three times "The light of Christ!" to announce the entrance of the Christ candle. After this, each person's candle is lit from the Christ candle until the entire church is aglow with candlelight. The celebrant then chants the powerful words of the *exultet,* which proclaims, "This is the night!" Again and again we hear the haunting proclamation, "This is the night!" This is the night when the blemish of sin was taken away. This is the night when Christ was victorious over sin and the grave. "This is the night!" Traditionally, in this service baptisms and confirmations take place. In this service there is also a beautiful retelling of the story of redemption from Scripture, with canticles sung by the choir.

Finally, on Sunday morning we return for the Great Feast of our Lord's Resurrection, in which we celebrate the fact that Jesus was raised from the dead.

What an awesome week is Holy Week. A week to reflect and embrace the mystery of the Cross upon which our Lord died, and the grave from which he was raised to new life again.

As a boy, every time I went to our family doctor's office I would race for that kaleidoscope. I loved the dazzling array of colors that awaited me, and the always-new arrangements I had not previously seen—a metaphor for life itself. Then one day the kaleidoscope was not on the table as usual. I was very distressed and asked the receptionist for it. She said, "Oh, it was used so long, it got stuck. You can only see one picture through it now." She handed me the scope. She was right. Changing the dial made no difference; the picture was stuck.

Life can be like that, too. We can get stuck emotionally in the pain of what it means to be human. For me, Holy Week is a way of getting our lives unstuck. In participating in the services of that amazing week, we experience the paradox of Christ's death and glorious resurrection. Participate in Holy Week, and the paradoxes of your own lives and the kaleidoscope of our own emotions can begin to take on new meaning. Let that happen, and you may never be the same.

Chapter 22

Friedman's Democratizations, Pentecost, and Jabez's Prayer

When the day of Pentecost had come, they were all together in one place. And suddenly from heaven there came a sound like the rush of a violent wind, and it filled the entire house where they were sitting. Divided tongues, as of fire, appeared among them, and a tongue rested on each of them. All of them were filled with the Holy Spirit and began to speak in other languages, as the Spirit gave them ability. (Acts 2:1-4)

*I*n 2001, a book entitled *The Prayer of Jabez* became a number-one best seller. Millions of copies were sold, and booksellers could hardly keep the book in stock. The subject of Bruce Wilkinson's little book is a short prayer by a rather obscure man named Jabez, who is recorded in 1 Chronicles in the Old Testament (4:9-10) and hidden in the middle of a long, six-chapter list of over 500 names, starting with Adam and Eve, and on down through history.

I must confess, I skip over lists like that when I read the Bible. Apparently the author doesn't, because that's where he found the prayer that Jabez prayed, asking for four things: (1) that God would bless him, (2) that God would enlarge his border or territory, (3) that God's hand would be upon him, and (4) that God would keep him from harm. The same verse says, "And God granted what he asked."

The question is, can we pray that prayer? I mean, can we ask God to bless us, extend our territory, put his hand upon us, and keep us out of harm's way? The fact is, most of us pray for ourselves only when we are sick or when catastrophe strikes. We are far more comfortable praying for other people or for God to bless our nation, as we do on Memorial Day. But to ask God to bless us personally seems inappropriate, presumptuous, and perhaps even prideful.

Yet, when you think about it, the prayer of Jabez was fulfilled on the day of Pentecost, when the glory of God fell upon the 120 disciples who waited for the promise of God in the Holy Spirit. God blessed the disciples that day, God's hand was upon them, and the church's influence has been extending ever since. And today, each year we celebrate the Day of Pentecost, the day the church was born and God's Holy Spirit came in power.

Something glorious happened that day, that's for sure. Thomas L. Friedman says something dramatic is taking place in our day, as well. Friedman is a foreign-affairs columnist for *The New York Times*. In his book *The Lexus and the Olive Tree,* he says that the world is undergoing a transformation so radical that world leaders, corporations, and individuals are scrambling to adjust to a new system of globalization, and he says that "you ain't seen nothing yet."[1] Friedman identifies three democratizations that have taken place in the last few decades—the democratization of technology, of finance, and of information. By *democratization,* Friedman means that technology, finance, and information are now in the hands of ordinary people to an extent previously unimaginable in all of human history. Friedman says this means that all the rules have changed, blowing away all the walls that separate people politically, economically, and culturally. Because of technology, this also means that the least among us has become "super-empowered." Today, on the Internet, you no longer need a passport to travel. Within seconds, any man, woman, or child can reach a vast network of people around the globe. A person living on a remote island in the South Pacific with an online laptop computer can start a company, distribute goods worldwide, and, in the process, might even scandalize the financial integrity of the largest corporation in America.

I mention Friedman's three democratizations because I believe democratization is precisely what Pentecost is all about. On the Day of Pentecost, all the rules changed. Everything became new. Walls were broken down, and old things passed away. Young men began to see visions that made them wise beyond their years. Old men who had long ago stopped dreaming about their future, suddenly began dreaming again, about how things ought to be. The Spirit of God fell on women,

---

1. Thomas L. Friedman, *The Lexus and the Olive Tree.* (New York: Anchor Books, a division of Doubleday, 2000), p. 139.

too—something unheard of in prior biblical history. Previously, God's Spirit fell only on men, but on the day of Pentecost, women were included, and not just women of high social status—women of low means received the blessing as well. Not just priests or members of the ruling class—all had flames of fire on their heads, and all were filled with the mighty power of God's Spirit. (See Acts 2:14-21.)

Jesus said that after the power of the Holy Spirit came upon his disciples, they would be his witnesses in Jerusalem, in Judea, in Samaria, and to the ends of the earth. After the Holy Spirit fell at Pentecost, Peter—a fisherman and a man who had denied Christ three times—began to preach, and 3,000 accepted Christ that day. From that day on, Jesus' disciples became witnesses to Christ wherever they went, to the ends of the earth, far from the Mount of Olives in Jerusalem, where Jesus gave his prophecy.

"Very truly, I tell you, the one who believes in me will also do the works that I do and, in fact, will do greater works than these," Jesus said (John 14:12). He reached a handful of common people—fishermen and tax collectors, for example. Yet these ordinary men and women, when filled with the power of God's Spirit, literally turned their world upside down, and ever since then, ordinary people—like you and me—have been carrying the gospel to the ends of the earth.

I have thought a lot about Jabez's prayer. I don't know about you, but I believe that Jabez's prayer could be *my* prayer. I have no problem asking God to bless me, to extend the border of my influence, to place his hand upon me, and to keep me from bringing harm to others. I would not be asking God to bless me with a Mercedes-Benz. Nor would I be asking God for great wealth; I cannot complain about what I have. No, when I pray the prayer of Jabez, I am asking God to bless me so that I can be a blessing to others, because without the blessing of God, it is impossible for me to bless anyone. When I ask God to place his hand upon me, I would be asking God to take my unruly heart and transform me into the image of God's dear Son. That's why I believe Jabez's prayer is a prayer we can all pray.

At Pentecost, God wanted to give the gifts of the Holy Spirit and to empower all people. But how do we receive the Holy Spirit? A little further in the second chapter of Acts, people asked Peter what they must do to be saved, and he told them, "Repent, and be baptized every one of you in the name of Jesus Christ so that your sins may be forgiven" (2:38). Then Peter said, "And you will receive the gift of the Holy Spirit. For the promise is for you, for your children, and for all who are far away, everyone whom the Lord our God calls to him" (2:38*b*-39). You have been called of God or you wouldn't be reading this book, so the promise of God belongs to you.

Talk about democratization! God calls people of all age groups and of every race, color, and creed—all are called; no one is excluded. God wants to fill us all with the power of his Holy Spirit. God wants to bless us and extend our territory by extending the influence of God's people and their witness, far and wide.

Perhaps you, like me, have seen or heard of the remarkable story of Nkosi Johnson of Johannesburg, South Africa. Nkosi was born in 1989 to a mother who was HIV-positive. Over 4.7 million people in South Africa are now carriers of the HIV virus. And because his mother did not receive the drugs that could have kept her child from becoming infected, this precious little boy was born with the virus in his bloodstream. His life expectancy was a mere three years. But Nkosi did not die at age three; instead, God extended his territory—his days on earth, if you will—and God extended the influence of this little boy as well.

Nkosi was blessed with a brilliant mind and a maturity far beyond his years, but his road was not easy. When he became seven years old and had not died, his foster mother, Gail Johnson, tried to enroll him in public school, only to be refused admission because of his illness. Nkosi's struggle to receive an education was widely publicized in the media of that country, which brought him into the public limelight. Eventually, his situation and his perseverance led to a national policy in South Africa banning discrimination against infected children.

Later, God opened the door for Nkosi to speak about his condition in television interviews, and when he proved so effective, at eleven years of age he appeared live on a global television broadcast. With an appealing smile and sparkling eyes, Nkosi touched the hearts of millions of people as he told how he had burst into tears when he learned his mother had died. He said he wished that the government would start giving AZT to pregnant HIV-positive mothers, to help stop the virus from being passed on to their babies. He told people that "you can't get AIDS if you touch, hug, kiss, or hold hands with someone who is infected." He pleaded for people to "care for us and accept us."

This little boy with a great big smile and a deadly disease awakened the people of the world. Soon help was coming from everywhere. An American donor paid for drug treatment for Nkosi, but by now his disease was too far advanced. Nkosi died on Friday, June 1, 2001. Finally responding in the wake of the public outcry for which Nkosi had given a voice and a face, the government of South Africa began to administer treatment to pregnant women with HIV.

Former South African President Nelson Mandela lauded Nkosi for his bravery, and he is being praised as a national hero. People around the globe mourned his death, as I did. In the fulfillment of one of his dreams, in 1999 Nkosi founded a care center, Nkosi's Haven, whose mission is the care of mothers with HIV/AIDS and their children. More centers are planned. Because of Nkosi, pharmaceutical companies have begun producing low-cost drugs to fight the disease, and agencies are collecting money around the globe to buy the medications so that no child will have to come into life with this horrible disease as their legacy.

Can God extend the border of our territory? Can God extend the sphere of our influence? Consider Nkosi, and I think you will know the answer to that question. God took the least likely person on the face of the earth—a little boy dying with AIDS in a developing country—God took Nkosi, extended his days, and extended his influence far beyond what anyone ever could have imagined. If God can do that with Nkosi, I wonder what can God do with you and me?

One thing is certain—today the democratization of technology, finance, and information is at hand, and with it all the rules have changed. And on the Day of Pentecost, all the rules changed as well. On that day we learned that God wants to do great things through every single man, woman, and child on earth. God wants to use all of us. That's what Pentecost is all about.

The question is, have we asked God to bless us and to fill us with the Holy Spirit? Have we asked God to extend the borders of our influence so that we might share the love of Christ with as many people as possible and be God's instrument on planet Earth? Have we asked God to place his hand upon us so that we may be transformed into God's disciple and harm no one? Have we asked God to bless us, so that we might be a blessing? I believe the prayer of Jabez is a prayer we can all pray. As for me, it's a prayer I intend to pray every day of my life.

Chapter 23

I Always Wanted to Be a Good Samaritan

Just then a lawyer stood up to test Jesus. "Teacher," he said, "what must I do to inherit eternal life?" He said to him, "What is written in the law? What do you read there?" He answered, "You shall love the Lord your God with all your heart, and with all your soul, and with all your strength, and with all your mind; and your neighbor as yourself." And he said to him, "You have given the right answer; do this, and you will live." But wanting to justify himself, he asked Jesus, "And who is my neighbor?" Jesus replied, "A man was going down from Jerusalem to Jericho, and fell into the hands of robbers, who stripped him, beat him, and went away, leaving him half dead. Now by chance a priest was going down that road; and when he saw him, he passed by on the other side. So likewise a Levite, when he came to the place and saw him, passed by on the other side. But a Samaritan while traveling came near him; and when he saw him, he was moved with pity. He went to him and bandaged his wounds, having poured oil and wine on them. Then he put him on his own animal, brought him to an inn, and took care of him. The next day he took out two denarii, gave them to the innkeeper, and said, 'Take care of him; and when I come back, I will repay you whatever more you spend.' Which of these three, do you think, was a neighbor to the man who fell into the hands of the robbers?" He said, "The one who showed him mercy." Jesus said to him, "Go and do likewise."

(Luke 10:25-37)

The story of the good Samaritan captured my imagination the first time I heard it preached in the little Methodist church of my youth. I recall sitting in the pew as our pastor, Brother Harrison, explained that the road from Jerusalem to Jericho was a treacherous downhill journey of winding roads. He said the terrain made it easy for thieves and robbers to hide behind rocks and pounce upon travelers passing by. This caught my little boy's attention, and I nervously imagined robbers pouncing on me.

With tension at the highest, Brother Harrison would then lean forward and say, "And folks, that's when Jesus comes into your life. When you need him the most, he comes and puts the oil of Gilead on your wounds, applies bandages, and takes you to the church where people can love you back to health." The contrast was so dramatic, I resolved with all my heart that I wanted to be a good Samaritan when I grew up, and to be like Jesus. I wanted to pick people up when they had been beaten up by the enemy and bring them to church so they could be healed and brought back to life again. I spent many hours imagining what it would be like to be a good Samaritan. Having said that, perhaps now you can appreciate how disappointed I was at my first attempt at being a good Samaritan in real life.

When our two oldest children were just two and four years of age, one beautiful spring day my wife, Pat, had gone off shopping, and I was left home to baby-sit the kids. Realizing I needed to wash my car, I walked our children, Kirk and Cathey, across the street and left them to play with some friends under a neighbor's supervision. I returned to my yard, picked up the hose, and began soaping down my car when suddenly I heard the screech of tires and a loud double *thud* coming from the direction of where I had just taken my two kids. I turned to see a small child lying behind a car in the middle of the street. I assumed the child was one of my children.

My many years of medical training did not prepare me for that moment. I have always been known to be the person you want to have around when trouble hits. Everyone says I am great in an emergency, but not that day. As I raced across the street my heart was screaming, *Why did you leave your children to go wash a car? Where are your priorities, John Graham?*

When I got to the car, I realized this was a boy from down the street and not Kirk or Cathey, but still I was so overcome with emotion that all I could do was just stare at the child lying before me. By now a crowd was beginning to gather, and someone said, "Look, a car is coming down the street." I said, "Look, a car is coming down the street." Someone else said, "It's coming too fast." I said, "It's coming too fast." Another said, "Better wave them down." I said, "Better wave them down." Next, someone said, "Look, he's not breathing." I said, "Look, he's not breathing." Someone else said, "Better do mouth-to-mouth." I said, "Better do mouth-to-mouth." But before I could begin mouth-to-mouth resuscitation, the child began to breathe and cough on his own. Then someone said, "We should call an ambulance." I said, "Call an ambulance." Next, someone said, "Look, his arm is broken!" I said, "His arm is broken." Another said, "Better make a splint." I said, "Better make a splint."

Moments later, someone showed up with two boards and gauze, and I began applying a splint. About that time I heard the siren of the ambulance, and soon an efficient emergency team took over. Moments later, the patient, his mother, and I were on our way to the hospital. As we raced to the hospital, the boy's mother grabbed me by the arm and said, "What would we ever have done without you?" My first chance to be a good Samaritan, and I was in such shock that I could only respond to what others told me to do. It was a most humbling experience for this physician.

The parable of the good Samaritan makes for powerful and inspiring preaching. But the more I think about it, the more I believe the central issue of the Scripture passage is when it says the lawyer wanted to justify himself when he asked Jesus, "Who is my neighbor?" Jesus had said that we are commanded to love our neighbor as we love ourselves (Luke 10:27). How did the lawyer excuse his disobedience? By saying, "I can't obey because I don't even know who my neighbor is."

The excuse was a lame one. Being a lawyer, he clearly understood the commands of the Jewish law: He was to love his neighbor as himself. And, that was his problem! His problem was the clear imperative of Scripture. And, that's *our* problem as well, isn't it? The Oklahoma comedian Will Rogers is said to have once said, "It's not what Scripture *doesn't* say that bothers me. It's what Scripture *does* say." That was this lawyer's problem, and it is ours as well. We know all too well what the Scriptures are saying—what God's will is in a situation.

So, to escape the clear command of God's Word, the lawyer tried to invalidate it by asking the question, "Who is my neighbor?" Jesus responded by telling a simple and yet powerful parable. In it, Jesus made clear that the real question is not "Who is my neighbor?" Rather, it is, "Am I being a good neighbor to those in need?"

By telling his parable Jesus held the man accountable. In fact he added to the demands of the law fourfold. Not only did the man's neighbor include fellow Jews; in Jesus' parable, the lawyer learned that his neighbor included anyone in need.

Not only that, but the gift must not be minimal. No, in Jesus' view, the provision should be extravagant. Look at all the Samaritan did. Giving lavishly is how to love one's neighbor as oneself.

Jesus didn't stop there. Love your *neighbor? That's* too hard? Elsewhere in Scripture, Jesus had said that not only should you love your neighbor, but you also should "love your enemies," and while you are at it, you should "pray for those who persecute you" (Matthew 5:44).

Then Jesus added the compelling imperative, "Be perfect, therefore, as your heavenly Father is perfect" (Matthew 5:48). He can't be serious! Is he calling us mere mortals to be like *God?*

Scripture says that our flesh lusts against the Spirit, and the fact is, few of us faithfully respond to God's call. We need the power of God's Holy Spirit in our life to lead, guide, and empower us to do his will. We also need one another, because just like the lawyer in Luke 10:25-37, we often refuse to allow the Holy Spirit to do his work in us. Let me share a story to illustrate how I know this is true of me.

Several years ago, while I was serving St. Matthew's church in Austin, Texas, I received a phone call from a man in Pennsylvania who asked me to perform a memorial service for his son-in-law. Over time, the young man had become unemployed and eventually had become involved in the distribution of drugs. Just two weeks prior to my receiving the call from his father-in-law, police had raided his apartment, and when he tried to defend himself, he was killed. Bullets missed the man's daughter by inches or she would be dead as well.

The man then told me the boy's parents lived in a nearby city and were members of another denomination. Their son's death had been widely publicized, and they had been unable to get a minister in any church to perform the service.

The man on the phone had assured the family he could find a church that would perform the service. Yet, though he had called several churches in Austin, he still had not found one that would grant his request. Finally, someone recommended he call St. Matthew's.

The man said that the family wanted the service performed on Friday, which happened to be my only day off. Immediately my mind began racing to think of a way out. I thought, *These people are not from*

*this church. I'll never see them again, and who would know if I said no?
I don't owe these folks anything. They are not "our" people. Besides, it's
my day off. Why should I have to work? Our rector is out of town, and
I'm overworked as it is. I've worked two weeks without a break. . . .*

The fact is, I wanted to stay in control, and I wanted to have my day
off. I was about to say no, when suddenly it was like the day that accident took place in front of my house years ago. Only now I was surrounded by the people of St. Matthew's, and I thought I heard them
saying, "Look, this family is hurting." And I heard myself saying,
"Look, this family is hurting." Then they said, "They have nowhere
else to turn," and I said, "They have nowhere else to turn." They said,
"These people are wounded," and I said, "These people are wounded."
Finally, I heard them say, "You can do the service," and I said to the
man on the phone, "I can do the service." The moment I said this,
something burst inside me, filling me with joy, and I knew there was no
place on earth I'd rather be on my day off than performing that service
for those people.

Over the years, I have learned that my fellow Christians are people
who open their hearts to those in need—those whom the enemy has
destroyed and left for dead, the outcast. I know innately that the people
of God would have performed that service, and I know that the people
of God expect no less of their clergy. In a way, the people of God are
holding me accountable without ever being present—only they are
present, aren't they?

On Friday of that week, some eighty people gathered in the sanctu-
ary of St. Matthew's. Being of another denominational background,
they entered with caution, but they were clearly blessed by the words
of our wonderful liturgy for the dead: "I am the resurrection and the
life, saith the Lord. He who believes in me, though he were dead, yet
shall he live."[1]

I felt I was being God's servant and—like Jesus—was pouring the
oil of Gilead and applying bandages to a wounded and hurting people.
They were total strangers, not "our" people. They were people in their
hour of desperate need. What a blessing that service was for me, as that
day I fulfilled my boyhood dream of being a good Samaritan.

---

1. *The Book of Common Prayer.* (New York: Church Hymnal Corporation, 1979),
p. 469.

Following the service, the man from Pennsylvania grabbed me by the arm as he walked out the door and said, "What would we ever have done without you?"

Come to think of it, Brother Harrison may be right after all. Life is a slippery slope filled with danger. The enemy of our soul often leads us astray. But what a joy it is to be among people who know God's truth. What a joy it is to be among people who encourage me to be faithful to God's Word. What a joy it is to be among people who won't let me live in deception, people who love me enough to hold me accountable, just as Jesus held the lawyer accountable in his day.

Yes, I truly want to be a good Samaritan. And for that to happen, I need God in my life; I need my church family, too. I suspect that we all do.

Chapter 24

Mind the Gap

[Jesus said,] "Do not be afraid, little flock, for it is your Father's good pleasure to give you the kingdom. Sell your possessions, and give alms. Make purses for yourselves that do not wear out, an unfailing treasure in heaven, where no thief comes near and no moth destroys. For where your treasure is, there your heart will be also. Be dressed for action and have your lamps lit; be like those who are waiting for their master to return from the wedding banquet, so that they may open the door for him as soon as he comes and knocks. Blessed are those slaves whom the master finds alert when he comes." (Luke 12:32-37a)

The founding rector of St. Martin's in Houston wrote a little book entitled *Windows: Reflections on a Life of Ministry.* In his book, Tom Bagby says this: "The baseball park is the only place in the world where a priest can shout at anyone, namely an umpire, in righteous indignation." (Perhaps that is why I love the game of baseball so much.) Tom goes on to say, "Because I am a man of great vision, I am given to questioning the eyesight of any umpire. I think a good umpire and a good priest have one thing in common: They both 'call them as they see them,' regardless of what other people think."[1] One thing is certain: Jesus calls them as he sees them, regardless of what other people think. In Luke's Gospel, Jesus does not mince words when he says, "Sell possessions and give to the poor. Provide purses for yourselves that will not wear out, a treasure in heaven that will not be exhausted" (12:33 NIV).

Biblical scholars have long recognized that each of the four Gospels portrays a unique aspect of Jesus. In Luke, Jesus is a compassionate

---

1. Tom Bagby, *Windows: Reflections on a Life of Ministry* (Allen, Tex.: Tabor Publishing, 1987), p. 39.

friend of the poor, the outcast, and the sinner. Jesus came to preach good news to the poor, to heal the brokenhearted, to preach deliverance to the captives, recovery of sight for the blind, and to set at liberty those who are oppressed. The primary setting for Jesus' ministry throughout Luke is mealtime. Jesus eats with his disciples and also with sinners. He eats with those who are rich and with those who are poor, the outcast. He dines with his enemies, the Pharisees, and with his friends as well. All are welcome; none is excluded at our Lord's Table. For Luke—who also wrote the book of Acts of the Apostles—to be a disciple of Jesus Christ is to model one's life after him. Jesus was compassionate toward the poor and oppressed, healed the sick, and forgave the sinner. Disciples are to do likewise and are to follow Jesus unconditionally. In Luke, Jesus' disciples left everything and followed Jesus.

At the very center of Luke's Gospel—at the very heart of his message—Luke recalled that Jesus comforted those who had left everything to follow him by saying, "Do not be afraid, little flock, for it is your Father's good pleasure to give you the kingdom" (12:32). Knowing Luke's portrait of Jesus, the sentence that follows should come as no surprise either: "Sell you possessions, and give alms. . . . [and you will have] an unfailing treasure in heaven. . . . For where your treasure is, there your heart will be also" (verses 33-34, adapted). Jesus was giving a word of encouragement and also a challenge to provide for the poor. Both are at the heart of Luke's message.

Since 1996, I have been a member of the board of St. Luke's, Episcopal Health Charities, a ministry to the poor and medically underserved in the diocese of Texas. The first time the board met, we members were asked to introduce ourselves, and tell something about why we were asked to be on the board. Next to me was Dr. David Low, Director of the Center for Society and Population Health at the University of Texas Health Care System. He said something that I will never forget. Dr. Low said, "Dozens of studies now show convincingly that population health is not so much affected by the availability of medical care or even the quality of medical care." I was stunned to hear a physician say this. In medical school, I had been taught that the health of people was dependent upon the availability and quality of medical care. Dr. Low went on, saying, "The greatest effect on health is the social and economic conditions people must live and work in every day of their life."

My immediate response was to say, "If what you are saying is true, Dr. Low, the implications are enormous." He smiled and said, "Yes, I know." The next day he sent me a book entitled *Why Are Some People Healthy and Others Not? The Determinants of Health of Populations.* It was the first of many books I have read about the societal determinants of health, the latest being a little book by Richard Wilkinson entitled *Mind the Gap.*

Having read these studies, I am now convinced that what matters most in terms of population health is the quality of our psychosocial environment. I am referring here to the quality of our relationships at home, at church, in the workplace, and in the communities where we live. This is not to deny the value of excellent medical care. We still need the best medical care possible when we are sick. But, what I am saying is that the psychological effect that stress has on people is enormous, and that nothing is more stressful than those who must live every day of their life in abject poverty while so many live in prosperity. It is the disparity that makes being poor so deadly.

But the principle does not apply just to those who are poor. Everyone's health is affected by how our relationships are structured in life, and the disparity between those who have the power, money, and status, and those who don't. Those at the bottom of the pecking order feel shamed and experience low self-esteem. They have no voice and little control over their life, something that is vital to health and wholeness. I believe the ability to make our own decisions and carry these out is part of what it means to be created in the image of God. Yet, in modern society, social structures in the home and the workplace are often hierarchical, where orders come from the top-down and power, status, and prestige are reserved for those at the top. Let that happen, and the needs of many will be neglected—thus "the gap" that Wilkinson writes about.

Please understand, the traditional top-down, high-authority style of leadership is not in itself evil. In fact, we need a strong, authoritative leader during times of crisis. But when it becomes the pattern for everyday life, a hierarchy tends to create an atmosphere of chronic anxiety and the fight or flight emotional response that results in competitiveness, conflict, and stress for all involved—including those who make it to the top and have to work so hard to remain there. Over time, chronic anxiety depletes the immune system and makes people vulnerable to disease. Western culture is built on a hierarchy of dominance; no wonder there are so many sick among us, even if we do live longer lives.

There is an alternative. At work, in the church, and in our households, we can be mindful of this "gap" between those who have power, prestige, and status, and those who don't. We can create communities of friendship that promote equality, mutuality, and respect. This is important, because we are social beings, and everyone needs friendship, acceptance, and affirmation if we are to survive and stay healthy. Participation in a church or civic organization can provide the opportunity to participate in communities of friendship, mutuality, and respect.

In Luke 12, Jesus is telling us not to get caught up in the world's rat race. Let others compete and take for themselves; God wants us to be givers, not takers. Jesus wants us to "mind the gap" and exclude no one from our circles of friendship. He wants us to respect the dignity of every human being and welcome all to our table.

We all have a sphere of influence. For many, their influence is largely in the home. For others, it is at work or in the neighborhood. For still others, their influence extends to the city, state, or nation. Whatever is our own sphere of influence, we are to do all in our power to see that inequality between the rich and the poor, and the gap between the powerful and powerless, is minimized. Giving alms doesn't have to mean keeping people on welfare rolls. It does mean doing all we can to be certain that the hope of those who are poor is not taken away. It does mean doing all we can to see that every child receives a good education. It does mean, in our sphere of influence, being certain that every person is valued, respected, and receives just wages. Jesus is telling us not to pattern our life after the world. Instead, he wants us to pattern our life after him. Do that, and, he says, we will be rich in God and have great treasure in heaven.

Recently, I met an eighty-five-year-old man who looked me straight in the eye and said, "I am the richest man you know." I smiled, and he said, "I have more friends than anyone I know." He went on to tell me his life's story and how everywhere he had been, he had made friends. "I have friends everywhere," he said, beaming. He told me that he had been retired for years, but that companies kept asking him to be a consultant for them. I said, "You must have a special skill." He replied, "Oh, no, I think they just like to have me around. I have a way of making everyone happy, from the janitor to the president of the company." Indeed, he may be the richest man I know.

In his book *Windows,* Tom Bagby also said, "In the early days of Houston, the power brokers were easily identified because most of them had gained their fortunes by 'pulling themselves up by their bootstraps,' and they never forgot their humble beginnings. They shared their time and money in worthy community causes."[2] Tom gave the example of a retirement home that had been given by a wealthy Houstonian for the use of poor African Americans. He had been asked to officiate at the dedication service. Tom said that after the ceremony, the man who had given the money stayed on the property much longer than necessary. "And the residents got the message. This man had a personal concern for each person in the home," Tom said. "It inspired me to know that there were men of wealth who cared about the needs of other people."

I have lived in Houston for over five years now, and that has been my experience, too—the people of St. Martin's church sharing their time, talent, and money to better the lot of all citizens of the city. Some serve on the boards of foundations. Others have built Habitat for Humanity houses, served in soup lines, feed those who are homeless, and helped countless people in need—and not only in this city, but also throughout the state, the country and far beyond the borders of this nation. Truly, they have given alms to the poor. It is not just what we do to help those outside our church. It is also important to practice mutuality inside our churches as well, by recognizing the needs of those who are sitting beside us Sunday after Sunday.

St. Martin's is not unique; every church and synagogue has engaged in one or another kind of giving. What I am saying is that churches and faith organizations are where these kinds of things are taking place, in every city and in every nation on earth.

Most of us must spend all week long in places where hierarchies of power and dominance reign. This is not true when we gather in the Lord's house. In God's house, we are all equal—all sinners—and yet at the same time we are all created in the image of God and, by the grace of God, are all saints. It has been said that "God does not call the qualified." Rather, "God qualifies the called." God has qualified you

2. Ibid., p. 19.

and me through his Son, Jesus Christ. That's why we can come with confidence to God, trusting not in ourselves, but in him. And with no pretenses we stand before God's altar—rich and poor, those who are powerful and those who have no power at all—side by side we kneel to receive our Lord Jesus Christ.

We attend church to ponder things eternal, to bring our gifts and offerings, and, as Tom Bagby says, we come because in church we can "call them as we see them, whatever [people] may think." We come to remind ourselves that what is of primary importance in life is not how much money we have in the bank, but whether we have helped extend the kingdom of God on earth. Reminding ourselves of this reality is how we keep our sanity in the midst of a cold, cruel world. It is also how we keep our lamps burning, as we await the coming return of our friend and Savior, Jesus Christ.

Chapter 25

Little Robert and Last Things

At that very time there were some present who told him about the Galileans whose blood Pilate had mingled with their sacrifices. He asked them, "Do you think that because these Galileans suffered in this way they were worse sinners than all other Galileans? No, I tell you; but unless you repent, you will all perish as they did. Or those eighteen who were killed when the tower of Siloam fell on them—do you think that they were worse offenders than all the others living in Jerusalem? No, I tell you; but unless you repent, you will all perish just as they did." Then he told this parable: "A man had a fig tree planted in his vineyard; and he came looking for fruit on it and found none. So he said to the gardener, 'See here! For three years I have come looking for fruit on this fig tree, and still I find none. Cut it down! Why should it be wasting the soil?' He replied, 'Sir, let it alone for one more year, until I dig around it and put manure on it. If it bears fruit next year, well and good; but if not, you can cut it down.'" (Luke 13:1-9)

*L*ast Things: the last thing you and I want to have said about us, matters of eternal significance. Luke 13:1-9 is divided into two parts. The first half tells about two tragedies where a large number of people lost their lives, and in the second half, Jesus tells the parable of the fig tree.

First, we are told that Pilate had killed many Galileans and mingled their blood with the blood of sheep and goats—a horrible thing to any Hebrew. Mixing human blood with that of animals would have defiled their bodies and implied that they were eternally damned. The other story is that of a tower that fell in Siloam, killing many people. Jesus asked the crowds if the sin of those who died was greater than anyone else. In other words, did these people die because they had great sin in their life? Was God punishing them for their sins?

The question is as ancient as the human race. The overarching theme of Luke's Gospel is the proclamation of the universal need of repentance and forgiveness of sins. In Luke, Jesus is always reminding his disciples that it is not just the notorious sinner who needs repentance. For Jesus, all have sinned, and all stand equally in need of repentance. Focus on the sins of other people, refuse to forgive their sin, and suddenly our sins are the ones that will not be forgiven.

In Jesus' eyes you cannot put people into categories—one, a grouping of sinners who will be punished with sickness, with poverty, and with ill fortune; and the other, a grouping of righteous people who will be blessed with good health, riches, and good fortune. Forget that way of thinking! The gospel message is that all have sinned and all need to repent.

The fact is, until Jesus Christ went to the cross, until he was crucified between two thieves, until our Lord and Savior felt the agony of spikes being driven through his hands and his feet, until he felt the spear pierce his side, until his blood was shed and poured to the ground, and until his blood was *mingled* with the blood of countless others who had been sacrificed on the cross in this same location before him, until Jesus, an innocent lamb, was slain, until that dark day, the concept seemed a valid one—that God punishes the sinner and rewards the good. But the moment Jesus died on that cross, that concept was dashed forever! For on Calvary, the One who was without sin suffered and died for the sin of the whole world. And because that happened, Jesus' disciples are forever freed from the ancient notion that prosperity and good health are evidence of divine favor, or that poverty and suffering are signs of divine wrath.

The Hyatts of Hornbeck, Louisiana, were a good family when tragedy struck their household on Maundy Thursday, 1977. They were hard-working people who lived in a modest home in the country with their two children, seven-year-old Brenda and four-year-old Robert. Every Sunday they attended a nearby church. They prayed before each meal, and they loved God.

In his spare time, Gerald Hyatt had restored an old tractor, and little Robert had watched the entire process—from breaking down the engine and replacing damaged parts to finally applying several coats of red paint. It was a beautiful restoration, and Gerald was always proud to show it to anyone who was interested.

When Gerald arrived home on that Maundy Thursday, a friend was waiting there for him to see his tractor. While the two men went to the front of the tractor where Gerald turned the hand crank and started the engine, little Robert made his way to the rear of the tractor. He had watched many times as his dad pushed the power take-off lever to start a little four-inch shaft turning. The shaft could not have hurt the little boy, except a tarpaulin had been placed over the seat to protect it from the rain, and soon the tarpaulin was wrapping around the power take-off shaft, which was turning. Moments later, Robert's left arm was caught in the tarpaulin, and his arm was severed above the elbow.

Gerald heard little Robert's screams, ran to the back of the tractor, and seeing the arm was amputated, grabbed up his son and ran to his truck, which was parked nearby. As Gerald opened the door of the truck, Robert said, "Don't forget my arm, Daddy." Gerald ran back to the tractor and looked for the arm but couldn't find it. Then he unwrapped the tarpaulin, and Robert's arm fell on the ground. Not wanting to look at it, Gerald held the severed limb behind him as he ran back to the truck, and not wanting his son to see it either, Gerald put the little arm under the front seat.

Not waiting for his wife, Gerald screamed for them to meet him at the nearest hospital, which was located in Many, Louisiana. He took off down first gravel then winding blacktop roads, and finally they arrived at the hospital. Moments later his wife, Linda, arrived to be told they would need to go to Shreveport, Louisiana, where they could try to replant Robert's arm.

It just so happened, by one of God's strange coincidences, that in the emergency room was a physician who lived a hundred miles away in another small town. He said, "I just read an article that told what to do in amputation injuries—pack the limb in ice, and, oh yes," he added, "wrap it in plastic first to avoid frostbite injury." Because this doctor happened to be in the emergency room at the time, they did exactly the right thing, and moments later the county sheriff was racing north to Shreveport with the little boy and his arm, packed in ice.

At the time, I had just gotten home and expected to have three days off for the Easter weekend. I arrived to find my wife, Pat, in the kitchen with our youngest son, Patrick, dyeing Easter eggs. The house had been beautifully decorated for Easter, and I told Pat how beautiful everything looked for our Sunday dinner with the family. I was exhausted from trying to cram five days of work into four days, and I had just stretched out on my favorite couch to rest, when the phone rang. It was Schumpert Hospital Emergency Room. The nurse on the phone let me know that a child whose arm had been amputated was being sent, and that Dr. Shelby had asked me to take the case.

Immediately I called Pat, and the first thing we did was pray together for the boy and his family. I then went to the ER, told them to notify the anesthesia and OR crews, gave them my microsurgical instruments, and asked them to phone me when my patient arrived.

My office was located directly across the street from the hospital. I went there to be alone and gather my thoughts. First, I pulled down an anatomy textbook and reviewed the anatomy of the upper arm. I rarely operated on that part of the body, so I took a few minutes to review the structures of the upper arm. Next, I reviewed the steps for micro-surgical re-plantation of an amputated part. I had replanted thumbs and fingers many times, but I had never seen an amputated arm. Nevertheless, the principles would be the same as replanting a finger and an arm.

After going over the steps of the operation in my mind, I began to pray for the little boy and his family. I prayed that God would gather together the surgical team and the anesthesiologist he wanted for this operation. I thanked God for giving the knowledge to do the surgery and asked him to give me the wisdom I would need for this to be a successful re-plantation.

When I finished praying, my eyes fell upon a plaque that hung in the hallway outside the door of my office. It was the first in a row of plaques I had hung telling the story of my educational experience— premedical training at Centenary College; Tulane, where I attended medical school; a residency in ear, nose, and throat; and finally, my residencies in plastic surgery in Miami and in Norfolk, Virginia.

When my eyes fell on the first plaque, I felt God speak into my spirit: "All of this training is for this operation today." I was surprised and said, "Okay, Lord, and may it be to your glory." Moments later, I heard a siren, and assuming that was my patient, I hastened across the street to find the emergency entrance of the hospital covered with television and newspaper crews. Two sheriff's cars had pulled into the entrance. One sheriff jumped out of the first car with a little boy wrapped in a blanket. I knew that would be my patient. Another sheriff got out of the second car and was carrying a bucket filled with ice. I knew the bucket would contain the little boy's arm.

I followed the sheriffs into the treatment room and immediately began unwrapping the blanket. I had expected the arm to be bandaged since it was being shipped from a hospital, but in their haste there was no bandage. Instead, what I saw was the stump of an arm with bone sticking out an inch, nerves hanging out six inches, clotted blood everywhere. I was so shocked by what I saw that I stood transfixed for a moment, with my eyes riveted on the devastating picture before me. I felt myself turn ice cold, and the thought went through my mind, *A moment ago in your office, you thought you heard God say that all your training was to prepare you for this operation. Who do you think you are? You will never be able to put this boy's arm back on!*

I was shaken as my eyes moved from the amputated stump up to the boy's shoulder, and then I was looking into the face of a little four-year-old boy who did not have the slightest fear registering on his face. Instantly, I was reminded of my own son whom I had left back home dyeing Easter eggs. The face of this little boy said it all: You are the doctor who is going to put my arm back on, aren't you?

Not able to withstand the child's gaze, I went over to the ice-filled bucket, and soon I was holding Robert's arm in my hands. With no blood flowing, it was cold and white, a dead "part." The child's forearm was bent slightly from having been wrapped in the tarpaulin. I handed the arm to a technician and asked him to X-ray it. As he took one look at the arm, he said, "Oh, God, no!" He blanched and almost fainted. The situation had that kind of impact on us all.

A moment later, an orthopedic surgeon bounded into the room and taking me aside, said, "John, we have never done this kind of surgery here in Shreveport, but they have in Louisville, Kentucky. That's where we should send him." I replied, "No, this is what I have been trained to do, and we need to get blood flowing as soon as we can if we want to save his limb." The orthopedist said, "Then, let's ask the parents what they want to do."

When they heard the options, the boy's father said, "If Louisville is the best place, then I want my boy to go to Louisville." I said, "Okay, Lord, it is yours now. I can't do anything else." I went to the phone to call the air ambulance, and the other doctor got on the phone to

Louisville. Moments later, he shouted, "Hold up, John; they say if anyone can do it here in Shreveport, it should be done here."

A few minutes later we were in the operating room. We divided into two teams. The orthopedic surgeon took the amputated arm, scrubbed it, and identified the nerves, arteries, and veins on that end. After the boy was asleep and prepped and draped, I began identifying the nerves, arteries, and veins on this end. A few minutes later we brought the two parts together, and the orthopedic surgeon attached the ends of the bones together with metal plates and screws. While he did that, I secured a vein from the little boy's groin and then began placing interposition vein grafts between each end of the brachial artery and as many veins as I could find.

When I could find no more veins to reattach, I said, "Well, it's time to take the clamps off the vessels and see if the limb will re-vascularize." Everyone gathered around the table to watch. The anesthesiologist stood up, and the circulating nurses and the orderly who had been outside gathered around as we took the clamps off the veins and finally off the arterial repair. For several minutes nothing happened. We were all getting worried when suddenly from the top down, the limb began to turn from stark white to pink. When we saw this, everyone in the OR lost their cool. We were shouting as if it were the Super Bowl and our team had scored the winning touchdown! It was the most exciting moment in all my years of surgical experience.

With the arm re-vascularized and out of danger, we spent the next few hours repairing the damaged nerves. The muscles were then approximated and the skin closed loosely. At four in the morning, we wheeled our prize patient into the intensive care unit, again with nurses and doctors clapping their approval.

This became the Easter story of 1977, as the media spread the news of a resurrection story of sorts when a dead part came back to life again. Two weeks later, when I was ready to discharge my patient, I picked up the small recorder and began dictating my usual formal discharge summary, which went something like this. "On April 7, 1977, a four-year-old boy was admitted to the hospital with total amputation of the arm above the elbow. He was taken to the operating room, where, using microsurgical techniques, the limb was . . . " Halfway through my summary, I put the dictating device down and went straight downstairs to the hospital administrator's office. I told Sister Mary Agnesita, the hospital administrator, that I felt we should have a service of celebration and thanksgiving to God before little Robert went home.

She agreed, and the next day we gathered in the auditorium of the hospital where we gave thanks to God for what had happened. I told the crowd that I felt like David must have felt on the road back to Jerusalem after battling the Philistines, because David did not say, "Look what we have done." No, he said, "Look what the Lord has done," and he danced before the Lord and gave praise to God for their victory that day. And, I said, that's what I want to do—I want to give God the glory for the success of Robert's operation.

I had not performed a miracle, I told the gathered crowd. I had simply done what I had been trained to do—use an operating microscope to repair severed arteries and veins. The real miracle was that a number of things had been done correctly, which ensured the success of Robert's operation. First, the limb was not left at the site of the injury, which so often happens in the haste of the moment. Second, a doctor who happened to be visiting the hospital in the town of Many, at the time, made sure the amputated limb was packed properly in ice. Third, the boy was sent to Shreveport. I had just arrived and was trained in microsurgery. At the time, there was no one with similar training in New Orleans, Lake Charles, or even Houston. If they had sent the boy in that direction, which was just as close as Shreveport, a successful re-plantation may not have taken place. I told the gathered crowd that I believe God had watched over little Robert at the time of his accident and guided each decision that was made. With tears in every eye, we closed the meeting singing "To God Be the Glory."

Since then it has been my joy and privilege to tell that story in churches and civic groups from one end of the United States to the other, and everywhere I have gone I have given God the glory. Over twenty years have passed since little Robert's surgery. He is now married and using his arm quite well. With all my heart I believe that all of my training was for that one operation that day, to bring honor and glory to my God.

That's what the parable of the fig tree is all about. Jesus wasn't pleased when the people were trying to point out sin in other people's lives. Even recognizing their own sin was not the ultimate issue, and to get at that, Jesus told the parable of the fig tree. If it did not bear fruit, the owner of the vineyard said, it was useless and should be cut down.

The gardener protested, however, and at the gardener's request, the master said he would allow the gardener to cultivate the soil around the tree, fertilize it, and water it. In one year, if the fig tree bore fruit, fine; and if not, it was to be cut down.

What is the "last thing" that will be said about you and me? I believe the last thing, that which is of eternal significance, is whether or not we have borne fruit for the kingdom of God (Luke 13:1-9). For me, there is only one way we will bear fruit for God's kingdom, and that is to begin by first making Jesus Lord of our life; and second, let God lead, guide, and direct us so we can be useful instruments of God's grace. Do this, and we will bear much fruit.

First things. Last things. I believe the first thing is to make Jesus Lord of my life and then seek to find God's will and do it. For me, that is what life is all about—making God my way, my truth, and my life. I want to put God first in my life, because if I do that, God will be the last thing in my life as well. After I am dead and gone, I pray that others will say I was a man who put the Lord first and last in my life. For Scripture says that if we put God first and last in our lives on the last day, we will hear God say, "Well done, good and faithful servant! . . . Come and share your master's happiness" (Matthew 25:21 NIV).

Questions for Reflection / Discussion

John D. Schroeder

Chapter 1

My Mother's Picture Window

1. Share a time when you witnessed the power of love healing a division. How did you feel? What did you learn from the experience?
2. What does it mean to "abide in Jesus," and how do you do it?
3. What miracles can happen when you open the window of your heart to love others? Give an example.
4. Reflect on / discuss and list ways to show Jesus' love to others.

Chapter 2

The Full Sun

1. What does it mean that Jesus is "a full Son"?
2. Recall a time when you experienced God in the glory of God's creation.
3. According to the author, the revealing of Christ to others is whose work? What part can Christians play?
4. In your own words, explain the meaning of Epiphany.

Chapter 3

Not Part-way, But *All* the Way In

1. Reflect on / discuss what it means to be "all the way in" to God. How does this happen?
2. What impressed you about the story of the ear operation? What did you learn from this story?

3. What sometimes prevents people from going "all the way in" to God? List some common roadblocks.
4. What can you miss if your heart is not always open to God? What does it take to have an open heart?

Chapter 4

Scrubbing a Few Pigs

1. According to the author, what is Jesus trying to say to us in the parable of the shrewd manager?
2. Reflect on / discuss how Christians can be good stewards.
3. What does it mean to quit scrubbing the "pigs" you accumulate in life? Give an example of a current or former "pig" in your life.
4. Explain how sometimes possessions can end up possessing us. List a few warning signs of this danger.

Chapter 5

Cupid's Bow and All

1. What lessons did Jesus want his disciples to learn from the parable of the sower?
2. Explain how in our own lives, "seeds" can fall into each of four different areas, as outlined in the parable and mentioned by the author. Give examples.
3. What do you believe the author meant by his statement that Truth ultimately has a way of being accepted?
4. Reflect on / discuss ways in which Christians can be faithful in sharing the gospel, the good news of Jesus Christ.

Chapter 6

My Sky King Decoder Ring

1. What did you learn about the Book of Revelation from reading this lesson?

2. What messages does the Book of Revelation have for us today?
3. How do you deal with fear, your own or that of your children, regarding the bad things of this world?
4. Reflect on / discuss the promises and messages of comfort included in this chapter.

Chapter 7

The Most "Importantest" Thing of All

1. What did Jesus teach about dealing with conflict?
2. What is triangulation, and how can it be avoided? What is the healthy alternative?
3. What ideas or strategies have helped you deal with conflict in the past? Give an example.
4. What is needed for reconciliation to occur? What's the first step? Why does that first step often seem so difficult to take? What ideas do you have for making it easier?

Chapter 8

Forrest Gump—Labeled and Discarded

1. Share some past or present labels you have been given. How do you feel about having these labels?
2. What causes us to label others? List reasons labels are harmful, and reflect on / discuss alternatives to labeling.
3. What is the difference between a description and a label? Give an example.
4. Reflect on / discuss the many labels Jesus was given. How are Christians labeled today?

Chapter 9

Too Numb to Feel

1. What is the worst pain you have experienced, how long did it last, and how did you cope with it?

2. In what ways was leprosy a societal problem in the days of Jesus? How did society respond to the disease, and what consequences did this have for those who had contracted it?
3. What are some causes and types of hurt? Reflect on / discuss how Christians can show mercy and bring healing to people who are hurting.
4. Of the Scripture story in Luke 17, the author says that while ten men were healed, only one man truly "saw" that he was healed; what does this mean?

Chapter 10

Cast Away and Advent

1. Share a time when you felt pressed and compressed in the pressure cooker of life. How did you react? What helped you cope with the situation?
2. Read Luke 1:5-38. According to the author, what do the different responses of Mary and Zechariah to news from the angel represent?
3. What similarities are there between the events in the movie *Cast Away* and the situation of Mary's pregnancy?
4. How do you know when God is working in your life and seeking to transform you? Are there any signs or symptoms?

Chapter 11

Chad Hammett and In-Between Time

1. Recall an episode in your life when you experienced "in-between" time. How did you feel, and how did you cope with it?
2. What positive outcomes can occur while you are waiting? How can in-between times be both bad and good?
3. How did the disciples make use of their in-between time? What do you think they were feeling?
4. How does Jesus' prayer in John 17 speak to those experiencing in-between times?

Chapter 12

Saints: Ordinary People Living Extraordinary Lives

1. Reflect on / discuss and list qualities of character that would describe a saint.
2. What motivates people to live extraordinary lives? Is there any one thing that prompts this? What part does God play?
3. In your own words, explain what it means to be a saint, and give an example of one.
4. What types of sacrifices do saints make? Do you have to sacrifice to be a saint? Explain.

Chapter 13

My Satellite TV, Resentment, and *The Green Mile*

1. Share a time when you experienced resentment, and tell how you dealt with it.
2. Reflect on / discuss the real causes of resentment. What feelings trigger it?
3. For what reasons, the author suggests, did the disciple John resent the stranger doing healings in Jesus' name?
4. Reflect on / discuss constructive ways to deal with resentment. What does God want us to do with these feelings?

Chapter 14

"Go-Forwards"

1. How do you become united with Jesus, and what happens when you do? How are you changed?
2. Why do you take Holy Communion? What happens when you do? How do you feel after the experience?
3. In what ways are Jesus and his followers "go-forwards"? What is the significance of a new name?
4. What does it mean to us that God has the final say over death?

Chapter 15

Yoko Ono's Wish Tree and Prayer

1. What is prayer, and how are we to use it? Reflect on / discuss elements of effective prayer.
2. Share a time when one of your prayers was answered.
3. What is the importance of knowing, when you pray, that you are one of God's children? What role does having confidence play in prayer?
4. "God will never reject us"; what is the significance of this statement?

Chapter 16

The Perfect Storm

1. Reflect on / discuss how God joins us in the storms of life, and what that means for us.
2. List and reflect on / discuss what you should do when you find yourself in the midst of one of life's storms. (The author mentions that he tries to do four things.)
3. Share a time when you found yourself in the midst of an unexpected storm. How did you feel? What did you do?
4. What lessons can be learned from Mark 4:35-41?

Chapter 17

There Is Snoring in the House

1. Share a time in your life when you were asleep to a situation.
2. Define what it means to be "spiritually asleep," and reflect on / discuss what causes this condition.
3. Why is it often difficult to "awaken" others or ourselves to a truth or situation?
4. Reflect on / discuss the ways in which God attempts to awaken us.

Chapter 18

Michael Crichton, Authenticity, and The Authentic One

1. In your own words, say what *authenticity* means to you, and give an example.
2. What qualities make Jesus authentic?
3. How is Jesus different from the kings of this world?
4. If you could go back in time and spend one day with Jesus during his ministry (prior to the Crucifixion), what day would it be, and why?

Chapter 19

I Was Taught to Doubt

1. Reflect on / share a time when you doubted or struggled with your Christian faith or an issue of faith.
2. Why is it good to doubt? What does it often take to turn doubt into belief?
3. How can you help doubters come to believe in Jesus Christ?
4. When you are in doubt about something, how do you search for the truth? Give an example.

Chapter 20

My Train Set, Lienhard's Engines of Our Ingenuity, and Forgiveness

1. Share a time when you practiced or tried to practice forgiveness. What motivated you? What was the outcome?
2. List things that prevent forgiveness or make it difficult for people to forgive someone.
3. Reflect on / discuss steps to forgiveness and how God can help us forgive others.
4. List some of the misconceptions and some of the truths about forgiveness.

Chapter 21

Dr. Rigby's Kaleidoscope and Holy Week

1. Reflect on / discuss the author's statement that "at one time or another, we all reject God and all that God represents."
2. What help has God given Christians to deal with what is referred to often in the New Testament as the weakness of the flesh?
3. What makes Holy Week, the week preceding Easter, special for you? Which days are most meaningful? What do you look forward to?
4. Share a bit of your kaleidoscope of life—a moment of pain and a moment of great joy. What are the benefits of life's being kaleidoscopic in nature?

Chapter 22

Friedman's Democratizations, Pentecost, and Jabez's Prayer

1. According to the author, in what way is the prayer of Jabez one that all people could pray?
2. How are democratization and Pentecost related? How did all the rules change on the Day of Pentecost?
3. What impressed you about the story of Nkosi?
4. Who has access to the power of the Holy Spirit, and how does one receive it?

Chapter 23

I Always Wanted to Be a Good Samaritan

1. Share a time when you acted as a good Samaritan or when a good Samaritan helped you.
2. Reflect on / discuss why the lawyer asked Jesus, "Who is my neighbor?" and how Christians are sometimes like that lawyer.
3. What sometimes prevents us from doing God's will? What is needed in order to act as a good Samaritan?
4. In what ways is Jesus our good Samaritan?

Chapter 24

Mind the Gap

1. In the Gospel of Luke, the author says, Jesus is uniquely portrayed as "a compassionate friend of the poor, the outcast, and the sinner." Use your Bible to find some examples in Luke that illustrate this aspect of Jesus, and reflect on / discuss how these examples relate to our lives today.
2. Reflect on / discuss how Christians should respond to inequity among people in society.
3. What does it mean to "mind the gap"? Give an example of how you personally can accomplish this.
4. Reflect on / discuss: What is of primary importance in life, and how do we get our priorities straight as Christians?

Chapter 25

Little Robert and Last Things

1. Reflect on / discuss the story of little Robert and the lessons it teaches.
2. How do Christians bring honor and glory to God in daily life?
3. Reflect on / discuss the parable of the fig tree and what it means for us today.
4. Reflect on / discuss what it means to put the Lord first and last in your life.